# OWNING THE DA$H

*Applying the Mindset of a Fitness Master to the Art of Family Financial Planning*

## ANTHONY DELAUNEY

CFP®, ChFC®, CRPC®, RICP®, BFA™

**www.mascotbooks.com**

*Owning the Dash*

Tax policies, contribution limits, retirement plans, and other policies surrounding finance are constantly changing. This book was written with 2018 guidelines in mind.

Certified Financial Planner Board of Standards Inc. owns the certification marks CFP®, CERTIFIED FINANCIAL PLANNER™, and federally registered CFP (with flame design) in the United States, which it awards to individuals who successfully complete CFP Board's initial and ongoing certification requirements.

**For more information, please contact:**
Mascot Books
620 Herndon Parkway #320
Herndon, VA 20170
info@mascotbooks.com

Library of Congress Control Number: 2018913125

CPSIA Code: PRFRE1218A
ISBN-13: 978-1-64307-272-2

Printed in Canada

In loving memory of my cousin, my friend, and my inspiration, Greg Plitt. Your legacy lives on.

# CONTENTS

# INTRODUCTION

*"You have one life to live. Why wait until tomorrow to start it?"*

**—GREG PLITT**

Have you ever known someone who made you question yourself? Someone who challenged your perception of personal achievement? Someone who inspired you to constantly push yourself forward and never be satisfied with past accomplishments? Did you ever take a moment to step back and ask why this person had such a profound influence on your life? What was it that separated them from all of the rest—money, fame, power, or position? Chances are that your respect for this person had nothing to do with these measurable benchmarks. It's far more likely that it had everything to do with their character.

The person could have been a coach, a teacher, a friend, a parent . . . The list is endless. Their influence had nothing to do with how much money they made, how many fans flocked to them, their good looks, or even their brilliant mind. Instead, you likely found yourself drawn to this person because of their undeniable commitment to their purpose in life. They knew who they were, and regardless of circumstance or conflict, they stayed true to themselves.

So what does character have to do with finance or, for that matter, fitness? After serving as a financial planner for families for the past 15 years, I can tell you that it has everything to do with both of these subjects, as well as most other critical decisions you will make for yourself and your family. This book serves as a guide and a stepping stone, a means to achieve your long-term financial dreams and also prepare you for the uncertainties you are likely to face along the way.

This guide, like any other tool, will serve little purpose if you're looking for a quick fix and are unwilling to commit. Just like starting a diet, not sticking to your game plan will likely result in feelings of frustration, anger, and regret. But there is good news! Unlike starting a diet and having to wait for results, following the strategies and guidelines in this book will result in immediate gratification. You will be able to see the fruits of your labor, and you will acquire peace of mind in knowing that you are on track to achieve your goals. In addition, this guide is designed for families, so you will not take the journey alone. You can walk the path with your loved ones, celebrating each other's successes and picking each other up when struggles and unforeseen circumstances arise.

## MY INSPIRATION

Let's return to the subject of character and that person who encouraged you to step outside of your comfort zone and work toward your full potential. For me, it was my cousin, George

Gregory Plitt Jr.—or Greg, to those who knew him. Growing up, Greg was just another young man trying to find his place in the world, but at a very early age, he came to understand that in order to find happiness in himself and satisfaction in his life, he needed to give himself fully to whatever endeavor he set his mind to.

This became evident during his preteen years when he started wrestling for his middle school team in Maryland. Greg believed that in order to become the best wrestler, he would need to train harder and smarter than everyone else. He wanted to be the best wrestler not just in the school or in the league or even in the state; he wanted to be the best in the nation. Before long, his family saw this young man who started wrestling in the 129-pound weight class morph into a solid machine of muscle. He studied the structure of the human body, nutrition, supplements, and technique, working constantly to improve his muscular fitness. By his senior year, this indestructible terminator barely squeezed into the 189-pound weight class; he finished his high school wrestling career achieving second place at the National Prep School Wrestling Championships.

Although his achievements were remarkable, they were not what drew me or others to him. Instead, it was his constant drive to push himself to the next level that made him so magnetic. Greg went on to graduate from the United States Military Academy at West Point, become an Army Ranger, and serve our military dutifully in South Korea. After serving in the military, he came back to the United States where, by happenstance, a modeling agent discovered him and introduced him to the world of professional fitness modeling. Greg's desire to prove himself quickly became evident as his chiseled physique graced more than 250 fitness magazine covers.

The next chapter in Greg's life was probably the most impressive. His passion to improve himself was equal to his passion to help drive others to achieve their full potential. Greg determined that the best way to share his knowledge and experience with others was to develop a website dedicated to helping members not only improve their bodies, but also share their stories and life questions. Greg would answer these questions with brutal honesty, always letting members know that "we are not here to judge one another but to support each other and drive one another to our own greatest potentials." Greg's fans loved him for his honesty. His family loved him for his honesty. We knew who he was, and no matter the circumstance, Greg always held true to himself and to his convictions.

It is through Greg's website that this book came to exist. After watching his videos, studying his life and fitness lessons, and applying them to my own life and profession, I came to an undeniable conclusion. The experiences and mindsets that I have encountered in the world of finance are strikingly similar to what we experience in the world of fitness. Within these pages, I share these similarities with you and give you the tools to shape your future to reflect your dreams and aspirations.

Each chapter of this book begins with an inspirational quote from either Greg or someone he admired—a nugget of wisdom that can be applied equally to fitness and to financial planning. I personally wish I had heeded them sooner. Greg and I were close as children, but as we aged, we moved apart both geographically and emotionally. He lived on the West Coast with all the freedoms of a single man; I settled in North Carolina with a wife and two kids. He was a risk-taker; I stuck to the familiar. He was his own boss; I was working my way up the career ladder. Our paths rarely crossed, and I had little desire to browse his website or hear about his latest accomplishments.

That all changed one Saturday morning in January 2015. My wife picked up the phone and handed it to me. On the other end of the line was my mother. Through held-back tears, she informed me that Greg had been in a train accident and died. My 37-year-old cousin, who was like a machine, impossible to destroy, had left us in a split second. He was doing a video shoot for a commercial and something had gone terribly wrong.

Fortunately, Greg gave me and all of his family and friends an incredible gift: his website. In developing it, Greg had worked with a videographer to create educational videos of his recommended workouts. He would provide answers to members' questions and discuss his own life experiences. He would highlight the life lessons that helped him to become the individual that many across the globe came to know, respect, and love. One of his most critical lessons was to embrace "the dash"—that marker between your birth and death dates. Greg explained that this is the time you are given to achieve your dreams and leave a legacy for the future, a legacy that others will remember and use as inspiration to embrace their own dash. He referred to this mindset as "owning the dash": essentially, taking control of your life and serving as a role model for others to follow.

As a gift to Greg's family, the videographer created a 20-minute video featuring many of Greg's best quotes and scenes from the site's video library. The first time I saw the video, it left me in awe. It left me inspired. It made me want to learn more. It made me miss my cousin, but at the same time, it gave me great joy in knowing that the lessons and the experiences of his life were not lost forever. A new world of education and motivation awaited me, and I could not wait to dive in.

Greg's lessons have helped me to own my own dash in both my life and my profession. They helped mold me into the husband, father, and advisor I am today. They drove me to leap into the unfamiliar world of finance and grow over the years to become skilled at comprehensive financial planning, helping hundreds of families achieve their financial dreams. I have helped couples conquer debt, acquire dream homes, send their children to college, survive unexpected life catastrophes, retire with confidence, and leave incredible legacies for their next generations. Greg's lessons have also encouraged me to consistently improve the quality and scope of my professional advice by acquiring the following professional certificates: CERTIFIED FINANCIAL PLANNER™ practitioner, Chartered Financial Consultant®, Retirement Income Certified Professional®, CHARTERED RETIREMENT PLANNING COUNSELOR℠, and Behavioral Financial Advisor™.

My goal is to never stop learning and my hope is that as you read this book, my financial planning advice combined with Greg's insights on life and fitness will awaken inside you the drive to achieve your own greatest potential and secure your family's future. As Greg would ask, "Why wait until tomorrow?" Let's get started!

## CHAPTER 1

# YOUR MINDSET

*"The clock is ticking. Are you becoming
the person you want to be?"*

**—GREG PLITT**

Growing up with a cousin who was always stronger than me, always smarter than me, and always willing to put me in my place left me often feeling inferior. I hated the feeling. I hated being worse at sports, uncoordinated and clumsy. I often despised how easy it was for Greg to stand out in a crowd, demand attention, and talk to pretty girls. He seemed to be a constant reminder of my failures and inadequacies, and I had not even made it to high school. I never saw Greg scared or struggling. He was one of the older cool kids, and I was not.

Sound familiar? I was living the life of almost every awkward kid in middle and high school. I could have easily turned my life into one of those sappy sitcoms or corny '80s movies. Greg just happened to be my antagonist, the stereotypical big brother. To make matters worse, he was family, so I knew we would see each other at every large family event, every holiday, every birthday, and so on. Can you imagine the feeling? Do you remember the last time someone made you feel inferior, stupid, or unnecessary?

Think back to how you might have felt the first time you walked into a new gym or attended a cardio fitness class. For many, it feels like walking into a world of judgment. Everyone is looking at you, studying you, watching to see what you are going to do. They are examining your outfit, your hair, your walk . . . if you make just one mistake, you are back to being that awkward boy or girl in middle school, struggling to fit in. And the worst part is that you are doing the exact same thing to all of them. You're examining them. You're comparing yourself to them, trying to figure out if and how this group is right for you.

It's instinctual. It's built into our DNA. It's fight or flight, and almost all of the time it is completely unnecessary. Yes, some people will study you and others may judge you, but their opinion of you has absolutely no bearing on who you are and who you want to be. Our parents struggle to teach us this lesson as kids, even as they experience the same subconscious challenges as adults. It's normal.

This was one of my first realizations when I started working as a financial planner. After meeting with prospect after prospect, I saw a trend: people did not like sharing information about their financial lives. To many of them it seemed like I was pulling back a curtain to reveal a world of poor decisions and regrets, even with young couples who were just starting to take the journey into adulthood. They were not used to talking about money. Their parents didn't talk to them about it, and they knew that it was impolite to ask. These prospective clients had just met me and still felt as though every financial decision they had made up to that point was being judged.

So here is takeaway number one from this book: no matter what advice you seek, no matter the profession, you should *never* fear that you are being judged. Some talking heads and infomercials out there say that financial planning is easy. I assure you that it is not. Professionals exist because many of the things that we need to do to improve our lives and care for our families are difficult and require a great deal of time and expertise. If you ever feel that you are being judged by any professional, whether it's a financial planner, a physical trainer, a family therapist, or a business coach, address the issue immediately or seek advice elsewhere. There truly is no such thing as a stupid question, especially when it comes to having a sincere desire to improve yourself and your family.

Overcoming this fear of judgment is the first major obstacle that you will need to tackle to advance toward any major goal in life. I struggle with it every day, constantly reminding myself to go beyond my comfort zone. In fact, I remember the first day I went to the gym after starting Greg's workout program. It felt like going for the first time. Sure, I knew how to lift weights and run on a treadmill, but now I was trying new machines and routines. I can remember discreetly watching the other guys in the weightlifting area, getting an assessment of each one and trying to determine where I fit in. Yes, I was subconsciously judging everyone else in the gym.

Some were stronger and looked like they knew exactly what they were doing. Others looked like it might have been their first time. The stronger ones were intimidating. I wanted to make sure that I never got in their way. In my mind, the gym was theirs, and I was just a peon trying to work my way up. One guy in particular had a physique that was similar to my cousin Greg's. Standing at about six feet, five inches, he pressed dumbbells that together weighed almost as much as I did. Nothing was more fun than setting up at the weight station next to him, using weights that were half as heavy as his.

I did not say a word to him during those first few months. The best time for me to get to the gym was around 5:30 a.m., before I had to head out to work. Every morning when I arrived, he was already there. It drove me nuts! I started to resent him. I didn't even know the guy, but I was already reverting back to the immature boy who needed to make excuses. I had a family. This guy probably didn't. I had a full-time job and ran my own business. Who knows what he did for a living or if he even worked.

I kept coming up with excuse after excuse as to why I struggled each day just to get to the gym while he seemed to be so good at sticking to his game plan. I was trying exercises that I had never done before, so it seemed that every day my body was sore and achy. I wanted to quit, and several times I almost did. But right when I was about to give up, I would close my eyes and see my cousin Greg shaking his head and yelling at me, "No excuses!"

One day, I built up the courage to speak to the mountain of muscle who had intimidated me those past few months. As he was finishing up his workout, our paths crossed. We briefly made eye contact, and I sputtered, "You know, every time I come here, I can almost guarantee that I am going to see you killing yourself on these machines. You're setting quite a high bar for me." I didn't know if I was going to get a reaction or if I even expected him to say anything in return. Instead of moving on, he stopped, smiled, and extended his hand. His response threw me a little off guard.

"No. No. No, man. You've been doing great," he said. "I've been watching you, and you are definitely pushing it. I'm Josh." He went on to say, "Yeah, it's so hard to get out here every morning. My body is not what it used to be, but we've got to keep pushing."

Josh and I talked for a few minutes and then he headed off. After he left, I stood there silently and in disbelief. For the past several months, all that I saw when I went to the gym was a giant mass of muscle, constantly intimidating me, constantly reminding me of my inferiorities. With one short conversation, that mass became a person—not just any person, but a decent human being. I soon learned that Josh was also married, had two young children close in age to mine, and worked full time. He also used to play football for the Buffalo Bills.

Moving forward, when I went to the gym I no longer arrived with a sense of hesitation or anxiety. Instead, I arrived with inspiration. I wanted to push harder. Josh wasn't judging me. He wanted me to be successful just as much as I did. I've often heard stories of people meeting professionals who are at the top of their game and being completely surprised at how nice and down-to-earth they are. Many of Greg's fans used to say the same about him after meeting him for the first time at a fitness expo. Based on my experiences, we all want each other to succeed. Even in writing this book, my hope is for you to be successful.

When you find yourself hesitating to move forward with a financial goal in your life, don't worry about others judging you. They shouldn't, and if they are true professionals, they won't. They do want you to succeed. Greg often said that people have a tendency to keep "war gaming" their goals, struggling to figure out the best way to approach them and waiting until just the right time before taking action. The right time never seems to come. The reality is that the right time is now. Why wait another day to begin addressing your goals for a secure, sustainable future?

## CHAPTER 2

# YOUR FOUNDATION: SETTING GOALS

*"Life isn't about waiting for the storm to
pass. It's about dancing in the rain."*

**—VIVIAN GREENE**

One of my earliest childhood memories of Greg took place
when I was about 10 years old. I was at his house with several
other cousins and we were all playing lacrosse in the backyard.
Growing up in Maryland, it almost seemed like a requirement to
be able to handle a lacrosse stick. Some kids would spend hours
pelting balls against brick walls to consistently improve their
skills, but I was the awkward, clumsy cousin. Playing lacrosse
felt like putting a big bull's-eye on my back and asking the family
to take target practice.

There I was one beautiful summer late afternoon, sweating
in the hot sun and just trying my best not to look like a fool. We

had our teams set for one final game, and the score was all tied up. This time Greg and I were on the same team. He had the ball and was charging toward the goal as the clock was about to run out. Nothing was going to stop him, but just as he was in firing distance, he paused and lobbed the ball in my direction.

I frantically jerked out of the way, missing the pass and not sure what to do next. "Pick up the ball," he roared at me as my other cousins started making their way in my direction. I fumbled with the stick to try and scoop up the ball. I had nearly picked it up when my cousin Jason slashed the stick out of my hand, sending the ball flying. Greg charged after it and quickly recovered. But instead of moving again toward the goal, he blasted past the other cousins and dropped the ball in my stick.

Standing there stunned, I looked up at him. "Now," he said, "take the damn shot." I had never taken a shot at the goal before. My hands shook and started to sweat. The other cousins were running toward me again with their sticks raised high. I looked up at Greg and lobbed the ball as hard as I could toward the goal. The ball sailed about 10 feet off and to the left.

I looked back at Greg, terrified at what he might say or do. He didn't speak a word. Instead, he charged after the ball, recovered it, and brought it right back to my stick. "Now do it again," he said, signaling to my other cousins to back off. I shot and again I missed. "Again," he repeated, after retrieving the ball. I missed. And then I missed again. I missed a total of about 10 times. Each time Greg retrieved the ball and showed me what I was doing wrong. I was humiliated.

At that moment, I hated Greg. My other cousins were watching me make a complete fool of myself, and he didn't seem to care. He just kept pushing, forcing me to get it right and showing me what I was doing wrong. I wanted to escape, but I knew that none of them would ever let me live that moment down. Finally, I gave up on trying to look cool, swallowed what little pride I had left, positioned myself in front of the goal, wound back, and shot a sharp zinger into the bottom left corner of the goal.

What followed felt like a full minute of silence. Finally, Greg looked at me, smiled, and then ran over to the goal to recover the ball. "Good game, guys," he said as he dropped his stick and ball on the ground. "Tony, I'd better see more shots like that in the future."

And that was it. We all made our way back into the house as if nothing had happened. No one said anything negative—we just returned to our usual activities. The rest of the family had no idea what had transpired, and soon my subconscious worries of ridicule and embarrassment faded from my mind.

That childhood memory sprung up almost instantaneously when I started watching Greg's initial workout videos on his website. He would talk to members who were visiting the site for the first time, many of whom had likely never tried a workout program before. Greg stressed to each of them the importance of not worrying about feeling judged. He also emphasized how critical it was to go into any workout program prepared, to know what you are doing and make sure that you are doing it correctly.

It was just like me trying to take a shot at that goal. Initially, I had no idea what I was doing. I could have taken shot after shot and never hit the goal. I hated Greg's instruction and being reminded each time of what I was doing wrong, but with each new attempt and Greg's guidance, I consistently improved my shot and eventually made the goal.

Trying to go into an intense physical workout without direction or structure is unproductive and oftentimes dangerous. As a society, most of us want the quick fix. We want to get the muscles as quickly as possible. We will try pills, programs, or any other means as long as it promises to give us the results we want now. But, as we discover time and time again, the quick fix almost never works. Whether it is in school, the gym, or even the checkbook, we are constantly reminded that we need to pay our dues.

I was fortunate to discover this reality early in my career. When I started as a financial advisor, I initially thought that the majority of my job responsibilities would be to handle investments and make people money. As the years passed, I came to understand that investments are only a small sliver of the critical responsibilities in the financial planning process. In fact, one of the most critical but often overlooked responsibilities is preparation. People want to achieve their financial goals, but they go into the process blind. It's similar to my standing in the yard with the lacrosse ball in my stick, having no idea what I was doing. People make careless mistakes that can send them way off their mark.

So what does it mean to be "prepared" when it comes to achieving your financial goals? The answer has four components. This chapter covers the two related to your mindset (purpose and plan of action); chapter 3 covers the two related to your financial realities (net worth and cash flow).

## YOUR PURPOSE

*"Stop looking into the past for your greatest moments. Know right now that you are building your greatest moment about to be."* —Greg Plitt

The first step is to take an assessment of what you actually want to accomplish. It is nearly impossible to achieve any goal without knowing what the goal truly is. It's like starting a diet without a weight target or going for a run without an end destination. Yes, you may initially lose some weight on your diet or feel successful as you start your run, but the sense of accomplishment is fleeting. You don't know if you are achieving success because you don't know what it is that you want to accomplish.

Setting goals does not always mean that you must achieve a target "amount." Setting goals can be as simple as recognizing personal or family commitments and sticking with those commitments. For example, instead of saying that I have to lose 20 pounds, I could say that I want to maintain a healthier lifestyle by drinking two glasses of water each day, going to the gym four times a week, and drinking soda only on weekends. When running, instead of saying that I am going to run three miles, I could plan to run at least 30 minutes every other day.

In the worlds of health, fitness, and finance, it is incredibly hard to create "final" targets. This may sound counterintuitive, but when you look deeper at each particular goal, you often find that the goal is constantly evolving.

Greg gave a perfect example of this understanding in the world of fitness. During an interview with several other bodybuilders and fitness models, he was asked about measuring success and knowing when you have achieved your goal. A couple of bodybuilders said that you were successful when you were holding the trophy at the end of a competition. Some fitness models said you were successful when you made the cover of a fitness magazine. Greg challenged all of them. He said, "I have made over 200 fitness magazine covers. Does that mean that I have achieved success?" Of the bodybuilders he asked, "Does having a little piece of plastic sitting on your shelf at home mean that you have achieved success? If so, why do you keep doing it? How many pieces of plastic do you need to get before you know you are now successful?"

The bodybuilders and fitness models could not dispute his logic. Goals should be measurable, but they should not be constrained. Did Michael Phelps decide to stop swimming after he won his first Olympic gold? Did Warren Buffett or Bill Gates or Mark Zuckerberg call it quits after they made their first billion? They did not, because their goals in life were not restricted to a dollar amount, an Olympic time, or any other limiting factor.

Your goals in the world of finance should be viewed in the same fashion. What do you want for yourself and your family? Do you want to own a home, have children, send your children to private schools and/or college, buy nice cars or a vacation home, give to charities, travel, and retire comfortably? What are the priorities in your life, and where do they fall? Where do you want to be later in life, and how important is it for you to get there?

Taking the time to discuss these goals with your spouse or partner is also essential. You may have conflicting goals, and that is absolutely fine. Marriage and relationships are full of compromise. Not discussing these goals means that you and your spouse are not on the same page and conflict is likely right around the corner. Discussing the goals does not mean that you are guaranteed to achieve them all, but at the very least it gives you a direction and a purpose. This discussion also allows you to prioritize.

Identifying which goals are most important to you and your family provides a solid foundation from which to start a comprehensive planning process. When I meet with clients for the first time, I ask them why they have decided to work with a financial planner at this stage in their lives. The answer often has to do with a recent event or experience. One client may have just observed how the death of an extended family member resulted in heartache and stress for that person's immediate family. Another client may have witnessed the frustration and sadness of a close friend unable to help her child with college tuition. Another client may have seen a colleague forced to retire earlier than expected and known that he was in no way prepared for what lay ahead.

The hard part about financial planning is that the timeline for many of these goals is fairly concrete, with little wiggle room to postpone or delay. That is why naming and prioritizing your goals sooner rather than later is so essential. Knowing where you want to be makes it much easier to work toward each goal.

Imagine a hypothetical young couple named Mike and Jessica. They are in their early 30s and have been married for three years. They have no children but hope to start a family soon. They own a home and have some investment accounts as well as several liabilities, including a mortgage. Mike and Jessica both work, make a gross household income of $105,000, and have medical and retirement benefits provided through their employers. They have not yet worked on developing a family budget.

Mike and Jessica sit down to discuss their goals, and they write out a list in the following prioritized order:

- Purchase a new car
- Purchase a new, bigger home
- Start a family (two kids, ideally)
- Protect our family
- Plan for retirement
- Plan for college
- Take vacations

This framework, while very basic, will help them work toward their goals. It will hold them accountable to their priorities. It will give them a structure for their future planning. With these goals, they can start to be more specific:

- Purchase a $25,000 car in a year
- Purchase a bigger home in two years
  » Build a down payment of $30,000
- Start a family (two kids, ideally)
  » Create a list of lump-sum expenses for a baby (crib, diapers, et cetera)
  » Get a sense of budget that would include at least one child
- Protect family
  » Have an emergency reserve for "what ifs"
  » Prepare a will
  » Make sure family goals still can be achieved if one of us dies or gets too sick to work
- Plan for retirement in our mid-60s with a lifestyle similar to what we have now
- Plan for funding public college (four years for each child)
- Create a budget that allows us to spend about $2,000 on vacations per year

How specific they decide to be is completely at their discretion, and the likelihood of the goals changing is almost absolute. One constant that affects all families is change. People move. Jobs shift. Circumstances evolve. Trying to plan with the assumption that things will stay constant is a recipe for failure. The biggest advantage of identifying and prioritizing your goals is that it gives you a sense of purpose and direction. You start to understand why you are saving, just like you understand why you are going to the gym or why you are choosing the salad over the slice of pizza.

Knowing *why* you are doing something gives it value and encourages you to continue. With families, this is an incredible blessing because you are creating a goal not just for yourself, but for your family. Your spouse is depending on you and working with you. Your children are depending on you. Your family members will encourage you and also hold you accountable! It is easy to give up on a goal when you think no one else is watching. With a family, someone is always watching and sharing in both your successes and your failures.

Ask older family members or friends who have engaged in financial planning, and they will likely say that they wish they had started when they were younger. You have time and health and youth on your side. The earlier that you start, the easier it is. Now the question is, How are you going to turn those goals into realities?

## YOUR PLAN OF ACTION

*"Life is a plan of action. If you don't have a plan, you become the plan of someone else's life. You're not running the day; the day is running you." —Greg Plitt*

After identifying their goals, many families next want to jump right into reviewing their investment portfolios to discuss how they are performing. This is the old mindset of how financial planning works. *In order to get on track for my goals, I have to make sure my investment accounts are allocated properly. I need to focus on fees and on my rate of return.*

Applying this same mindset to fitness would be like going to meet with a fitness trainer, flexing your bicep, and saying, "I want you to make this twice as large." The fitness instructor could take the simple approach of walking you over to the dumbbells, putting one in your hand, and showing you how to curl it up to your chest. That would be it. You now know how to make your biceps get bigger, and if you stick with that game plan, you may end up having the largest biceps in the gym. The biceps might look good, but what about your chest, back, shoulders, legs, cardiovascular health, and diet? They would all suffer as a result of your limited focus.

Instead of walking you directly over to the weights, it's likely that the trainer would first get a better understanding of what you are trying to accomplish. Then he or she would take an assessment of where you are right now. When Greg introduced new members to his website, he would encourage them to measure their weight and the size of their neck, arms, chest, stomach, hips, and calves. He would recommend that they meet with a doctor to get a basic physical assessment to confirm that their hearts and bodies were in proper condition to begin a fitness regimen. He also would recommend that they meet with a fitness instructor to get a tutorial of how all the machines worked at their gym.

It was all boring advice. None of us wants to take the time

to develop an informed plan of action. We want results now. We want to address our goals now. Many people in both fitness and finance tend to skip the boring steps. They seem to be an unnecessary obstacle getting in the way of success.

However, those who have achieved success in finance, fitness, and most other walks of life will tell you that these foundations are essential. Jumping into a program without knowing where you stand leads to injury, loss, and often embarrassment. Understanding your foundation gives you a starting point and helps you to recognize your potential and your limitations.

In finance, understanding your foundation means taking a full assessment of where your family is right now. I stress the word *family* because this is an exercise in putting all cards on the table. Many spouses have little to no idea what investments or debts their partners have. Even after marriage, they keep everything separate. They convince themselves that their partner will get his or her own problems figured out and that they have no business meddling with the other's personal finances.

Please understand that there is nothing wrong with keeping accounts and bills separate, but as a family you are now working together as a team. Your decisions affect one another and anyone who depends on you.

When it comes to money, many families subconsciously—or oftentimes, consciously—try to stay ignorant of their current financial situation. We tell ourselves that it's better not to know how much we truly owe because knowing will just make us depressed and angry. It also won't change anything. We convince ourselves that something beyond our control is going to fix the situation. We say things like, "I'm not saving now because I don't make enough money, but when I make more money, I'll start saving then," or "I'm not going to look at how much interest I'm paying on my credit card because I don't have any desire to put more money toward that card," or "I guess I'll just work until I die. I don't have time to try and track all of this stuff!"

Time is probably the best excuse of them all. We convince ourselves that, one day in the future, life is going to settle down, that we will wake up one morning and magically have extra hours in the day to accomplish everything on our to-do lists. After all, it has to get easier after we get married, after we buy our first home, after we have our first child, after we change jobs, after we have our third child, after we buy our second home, after our children graduate high school or college, after we retire . . . In reality, life is a constantly evolving landscape, and it never seems to slow down. Free time comes only to those who work to achieve it.

So why wait another day? Once you know where you want to go, you need to assess where you are.

**CHAPTER 3**

# YOUR FOUNDATION: THE NUMBERS

*"To know where we are, we must first know where we've been!"*

**—GREG PLITT**

To assess where you are in life, you first need to understand *the numbers*. Numbers can apply to almost any goal you set. When you start a diet, you can count your calories. When you exercise, you can count your reps; you can measure your waist size, arm size, and chest. When visiting the doctor, you can measure your blood pressure, cholesterol levels, and body temperature. All of these numbers give you a starting point from which to develop a game plan.

In finance, there are two key tracking tools that can help you develop your family's financial foundation. These tools are your net worth statement and your cash flow statement.

## YOUR NET WORTH

*"Once you know where your current limits are, then you know
how to destroy them, push them . . . grow them." —Greg Plitt*

Let's start with identifying your combined assets and liabilities
(debts), otherwise known as determining your net worth. In
simple terms, your net worth is equal to the combined value
of your assets minus the combined value of your liabilities. It is
the report card that helps you determine your current financial
strength and the areas where you can most improve.

Clients often ask, "How good is my net worth? How does
it compare to others in my age group?" While understanding
where you stand in relation to your peers can be interesting,
comparing yourself to others is somewhat meaningless and
usually creates more problems than benefits. What other people
have and what you have are completely independent of each
other. This understanding is true in fitness, in finance, and
in life. There will always be people stronger and weaker than
you, fatter and skinnier, smarter and less educated, wealthier
and poorer. Their position in life has nothing to do with your
personal and family goals or your ability to achieve them.

Think back to the example of my friend Josh at the gym.
When I first met Josh, his physical "net worth" was significantly better than mine. Did that prohibit me from being
able to work out and progress toward my goals? No, but what
did limit my ability and desire were my personal feelings of
pity, frustration, and despair, realizing that he was so much
farther ahead than me. It was not until I recognized my own
self-destructive nature in constantly comparing myself to Josh
that I was able to retrain my focus and really start progressing
toward my personal fitness goals.

Your net worth is only a number. It's a tool to help you know your starting point and track your progress. The biggest benefit of a net worth statement is that it gives you an opportunity to see everything that you own and owe on one sheet of paper. Listing all of your assets (including your checking and savings accounts, your investment accounts, your personal property, your cars, et cetera) as well as all of your liabilities (including your mortgage, home equity loan, auto loans, student loans, credit card loans, and personal loans) gives you a very real sense of where you stand.

Recall the hypothetical couple from chapter 2, Mike and Jessica, who wrote out their financial goals. Assume that they have made progress by starting to save for retirement and future educational needs. The following net worth statement gives us a snapshot of their current financial standing.

## MIKE AND JESSICA'S NET WORTH STATEMENT

| TYPE | AMOUNT |
|---|---|
| **ASSETS** | |
| Checking Account | $1,000 |
| Savings Account | $4,000 |
| Work 401(k) Plan (M) | $10,000 |
| Retirement Plan (J) | $5,000 |
| House | $250,000 |
| Car | $20,000 |
| IRA (J) | $10,000 |
| 529 Plan | $2,000 |
| Joint Investment Account | $24,000 |
| **TOTAL ASSETS** | $326,000 |
| | |
| **LIABILITIES** | |
| Mortgage | $200,000 |
| Auto Loan | $10,000 |
| Student Loan | $8,000 |
| Credit Card Balance | $3,000 |
| **TOTAL LIABILITIES** | $221,000 |
| **NET WORTH** | $105,000 ($326,000 – $221,000) |

As you work to create your own net worth statement, I encourage you to take two extra steps. First, add a column for the *purpose* of each asset. As discussed in chapter 2, everything that you do in your financial life should have a purpose. Having an account without a purpose makes it almost impossible to determine what you should be doing with that account. Second, add a column for the *estimated rate of return*. In this section, write down the estimated return you get from each of your assets and the interest rates that you pay on each of your liabilities. Identifying the rate of return is easier for some accounts (like checking and savings) than for others (like investment accounts). For the latter, use this model, taking into account how soon you will need access to the money:

| TIME HORIZON | RETURN RANGE |
|---|---|
| Less than three years | 0%–3% |
| Two to five years | 2%–4% |
| Five to ten years | 4%–6% |
| Ten-plus years | 7%–10% |

## MIKE AND JESSICA'S NET WORTH STATEMENT (INCLUDING PURPOSE AND ESTIMATED RATE OF RETURN)

| ASSETS | | | |
|---|---|---|---|
| TYPE | AMOUNT | EST. RATE OF RETURN | PURPOSE |
| Checking Account | $1,000 | .06% | Cash Reserve |
| Savings Account | $4,000 | .1% | Cash Reserve |
| Work 401(k) Plan (M) | $10,000 | 7%–10% | Retirement |
| Retirement Plan (J) | $5,000 | 7%–10% | Retirement |
| IRA (J) | $10,000 | 7%–10% | Retirement |
| 529 Plan | $2,000 | 7%–10% | Education |
| Joint Investment Account | $24,000 | 7%–10% | Education |
| House | $250,000 | n/a | Personal |
| Car | $20,000 | n/a | Personal |
| TOTAL ASSETS | $326,000 | | |

*table continued on next page*

| LIABILITIES | | |
| --- | --- | --- |
| TYPE | AMOUNT | INTEREST CHARGED |
| Mortgage | $200,000 | 4% |
| Auto Loan | $10,000 | 4.9% |
| Student Loan | $8,000 | 8% |
| Credit Card Balance | $3,000 | 18% |
| TOTAL LIABILITIES | $221,000 | |
| NET WORTH | $105,000 ($326,000 – $221,000) | |

Do you notice any immediate red flags? Many individuals are so concerned with their investments and their rate of return that they tend to overlook unique opportunities to quickly improve their financial situations. For example, while putting more money into retirement and education accounts could be a great strategy, paying off their credit card at 18 percent and student loan balance at 8 percent could end up saving Mike and Jessica a significant amount more and would also help to free up their cash flow.

Creating a detailed net worth statement will enable you to make the same kind of evaluations. By being able to see everything clearly, you give yourself and your family an immediate advantage.

## YOUR CASH FLOW

*"When you have a purpose for every action,*
*every action has a result." —Greg Plitt*

Your net worth is only part of the foundation of your plan. The other part is your cash flow, and for many it is even more complicated than your net worth. One reason people are usually unwilling to meet with a money coach or financial advisor is that they don't want someone else telling them how to spend their money or judging their spending habits. But it's not always the advisor that people fear. For many couples, it's their spouses or partners who seem to judge or ridicule. "You spend *how much* on golf?" one spouse might say. "Almost as much as you spend on shoes," the other might reply. "Well, at least it's not nearly as much as you spend on beer and wine."

This volley of insults leads to nothing productive. Instead, it reinforces a couple's desire to never bring up cash flow to one another until major problems emerge. Once the debt starts piling up, it becomes a blame game instead of a strategy session.

Many families try to develop a budget by identifying all of their expenses and seeing where all of the money is going. I consider this a *bottom-up* approach to cash flow management. While it is helpful, it can also become cumbersome and exhausting. Most families with two working parents and one or more children will tell you that the expenses can change dramatically from month to month and year to year. Some expenses are seasonal. Others are circumstantial.

Using a fitness analogy, imagine a trainer instructing you to count all of your calories or all of your steps per day or the number of hours at your desk each week. While this information is interesting and helpful, it alone gives little guidance. It may tell you that you eat too much or that you need to work out or that you need to move around. But you already know that you are out of shape. Having statistics that prove it does not change the situation.

The idea of counting calories may sound good in theory. As individuals, we may find success in limiting our diets and sticking to certain food groups, but with families, one person's plan cannot rule all. If you tell your spouse and children, "We are eating only tuna fish and spinach from now on" without asking their opinions, this announcement is likely to be met with annoyed and angry looks. It is also likely to backfire. Before you know it, everyone is sneaking food and not joining you at the dinner table. They may even start to resent you.

What if you switched gears? What if instead of telling the family what they had to do, you instead had a sit-down discussion about both family and personal health goals? My cousin Greg often said, "When you have a purpose for every action, every action has a result." When your family has a communal purpose for making changes in their eating habits—such as eating nutrient-rich food to improve everyone's energy levels—it becomes far easier to achieve. It also provides a support system wherein you all know the game plan, and you are there to encourage one another.

In the world of finance, I have discovered that my most successful and financially stable families learn very quickly that viewing their cash flow and spending habits from a *top-down* approach is significantly more efficient and easier to stick to. So what does it mean to use a top-down approach? It means that you are giving a purpose to each cash outflow that you have.

After breaking down your expenses, you can direct your outgoing cash flow info four separate categories:

- Committed expenses
- Taxes
- Savings
- Discretionary (fun money) spending

Two of these categories are usually easy to identify and determine: committed expenses and taxes. With taxes, for example, you can identify your vehicle and property taxes. You can also determine your family's *taxable* income and estimate your total federal, state, and FICA (Social Security and Medicare) taxes for the year. If you don't know how to determine your taxable income, ask your tax advisor to walk you through the process or review your previous year's 1040 tax statements. The taxable income is listed on page two, line 43, of the form. If you do not have a tax advisor, there are many free online calculators that can help with this process. The importance of knowing your taxable income and how it is calculated will be discussed in chapter 5.

While there is some wiggle room with adjusting the taxes that you owe (see chapter 5), overall they are straightforward calculations. The same can be said for your committed expenses. Start by looking at your pay stub. Expenses pulled from the pay stub—including medical, dental, and vision insurance—are usually constant. In addition, expenses like utilities, grocery bills, and liability payments remain fairly stable and easy to identify.

While these expenses are considered essential, there are others that many would argue also fit into this category given the service-based environment in which we now live. Consider viewing all your committed expenses as either primary (essential) or secondary (important but not vital). For example:

**Primary Committed**
- Liabilities—mortgage, auto loan, student loan, et cetera
- Medical insurance
- Medical copays and deductibles
- Auto and home insurance
- Utility bills (electric, gas, water, trash)
- Grocery bills (including household items like toiletries)

- Auto fuel
- Auto maintenance
- Basic clothing
- Homeowners' association dues (if applicable)

**Secondary Committed**
- Home/cell phones
- Internet service
- Personal care
- Home repair
- Charitable giving
- Pet expenses

Once you have identified your income(s), taxes, and committed expenses, you then have a choice. You can choose to focus on your savings needs, or you can instead identify your discretionary (fun money) expenses. Here is where I differentiate between the top-down and bottom-up approaches.

Creating a budget based on current spending habits is a path to nowhere. It shows that you prioritize what you have now over your goals for the future. It would be like walking up to a fitness instructor and stating that you want her to help you get into incredible shape, but you are very concerned about not being able to eat ice cream after dinner, smoke five cigarettes per day, drink three beers at night, and enjoy other habits and rituals that you already know are hindering your ability to be fit.

Instead of focusing on where you are now and what you will lose, focus on your priorities. Greg loved to say, "Keep your mind focused on the horizon. Don't get carried away with all of the speedbumps in life. Eye on the horizon of your future.

You will be there soon enough!" In finance, this means that you should prioritize the savings part of your cash flow before you get too caught up with all of the discretionary spending *wants*.

It is not as difficult as it may sound. Many of us have heard the phrase "Money not seen is money not missed." It's amazing how the psychology of money works. There are individuals who make $30,000 a year and still have extra money to spend, and there are individuals who make over $250,000 a year and feel like they are pinching pennies. It all depends on their priorities. If you start with your goals in mind and dedicate your cash flow accordingly, you achieve the peace of mind of knowing that the money you are not spending is now going toward a purpose. It is helping ensure that your priorities can be achieved. It's a matter of determining what you need to do to make those goals a reality.

Let's return to Mike and Jessica. Their annual cash flow statement is below:

### ANNUAL CASH FLOW STATEMENT FOR MIKE AND JESSICA

| TYPE | AMOUNT |
| --- | --- |
| INCOMES | |
| Salary (Mike) | $45,000 |
| Salary (Jessica) | $55,000 |
| Bonus (Mike) | $5,000 |
| TOTAL INCOME | $105,000 |

*table continued on next page*

## PRIMARY COMMITTED EXPENSES

| | |
|---|---|
| Mortgage | $12,000 |
| Auto loan | $6,000 |
| Student loan | $3,000 |
| Credit card minimum payment | $600 |
| Medical insurance | $6,000 |
| Medical copays and deductibles | $2,600 |
| Auto insurance | $1,500 |
| Home insurance | $800 |
| Utility bills (electric, gas, water, trash) | $3,000 |
| Grocery bills | $7,200 |
| Auto fuel | $3,000 |
| Auto maintenance | $1,000 |
| Basic clothing | $2,000 |
| Personal care | $300 |
| Homeowners' association dues | $750 |
| **TOTAL PRIMARY COMMITTED** | **$49,750** |

## SECONDARY COMMITTED EXPENSES

| | |
|---|---|
| Home/cell phones | $1,440 |
| Internet service | $400 |
| Home repair | $500 |
| Alarm system | $600 |
| Pet expenses | $500 |
| Charitable giving | $3,000 |
| **TOTAL SECONDARY COMMITTED** | **$6,440** |

| TAXES (MARRIED FILING JOINTLY) | |
|---|---|
| Federal income tax | $8,619 |
| State income tax | $5,053 |
| Social Security tax | $6,510 |
| Medicare tax | $1,523 |
| Property tax | $1,200 |
| Vehicle tax | $300 |
| **TOTAL TAXES** | **$23,205** |
| **TOTAL COMMITTED EXPENSES & TAXES** | **$79,395** |
| **AVAILABLE FUNDS FOR SAVING / DISCRETIONARY SPENDING** | **$25,605 ($105,000 – $79,395)** |

| SAVINGS / PROTECTION GOALS | |
|---|---|
| Retirement | ? |
| Education | ? |
| Protection | ? |
| New car | ? |
| New home | ? |
| **TOTAL SAVINGS / PROTECTION** | **$?** |

| DISCRETIONARY SPENDING | |
|---|---|
| Dining and recreation | ? |
| Vacations | ? |
| Gym memberships | ? |
| Gifts to family | ? |
| Video streaming service | ? |
| **TOTAL DISCRETIONARY SPENDING** | **$?** |
| **REMAINING CASH FLOW** | **$?** |

You may have noticed a series of question marks listed next to all of the savings and protection goals as well as the discretionary spending expenses. You also may have noticed that the savings and protection goals are listed above the discretionary expenses. Setting up your cash flow in this fashion forces you and your spouse to make a decision. Based on the information provided, you know what funds are available to put toward the remaining savings and discretionary spending categories. In the sample cash flow, Mike and Jessica have $25,605 in remaining cash flow. Now they have to choose which category, Savings/Protection or Discretionary Spending, they will address first.

This step in the planning process is the hardest obstacle for most people to overcome. Trying to plan for your life in 5, 10, 20, or 30-plus years is extremely difficult to do. It is even harder when you are planning for other people's lives. Some questions are impossible to know the exact answer to: How much will we need for a down payment on our new home? What should we expect for our kids' college education expenses in 20 years? What will our family budget look like when we retire?

Advances in technology have made the process even more challenging, especially when it comes to retirement planning. Our grandparents' golden years were nothing like what we will likely experience in our own retirements. When we imagine retirements for previous generations, we often envision rocking chairs on wraparound porches, card games, baked apple pies, sitcoms on the TV, and grandchildren playing nearby.

Our grandparents' retirement seemed simple and easy, and in many ways it was. Try to imagine the cash flow statements of the generations before us. Now envision your own current cash flow statement. What didn't exist 30 years ago is now a staple or committed expense in your life: cell phones, data packages, internet bill, cable TV, alarm system, timeshare, Netflix . . . the list could go on and on. We have become a society of services, and while these services are wonderful and may improve the quality of our lives, they are still expenses that will continue to rise with inflation throughout our retirements.

So here is where you and your partner need to make a critical decision. Are you going to stay true to your priorities, or are you going to allow your immediate discretionary wants to sabotage your future goals?

Once you have identified your goals and priorities and determined your income(s), taxes, and committed expenses, the next step is to systematize. Don't give yourself the option, or more specifically the temptation, to stray from your commitments.

In all of my years working as an advisor, I have discovered that the following chart is one of the most vital approaches to cash flow management. Using it separates successful clients from those who seem to consistently run into financial complications. The breakdown shows a cash flow system where if you work from the top down, you are forced to stick to your priorities. You are also given a clearer understanding of where your money is going and how much you truly have left to dedicate toward your discretionary wants.

# TOP-DOWN CASH FLOW BREAKDOWN

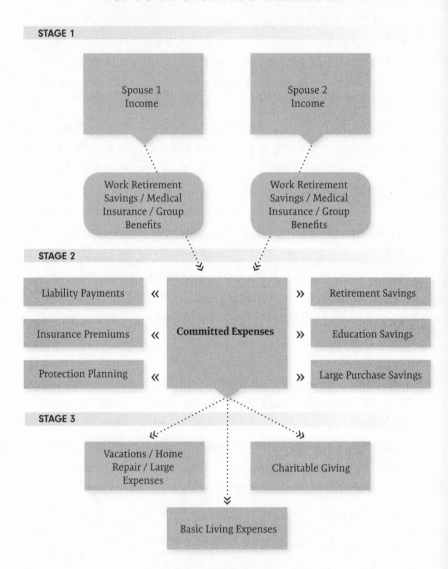

After applying these steps to the incomes and expenses listed in the sample cash flow statement, the chart would be updated to look like this:

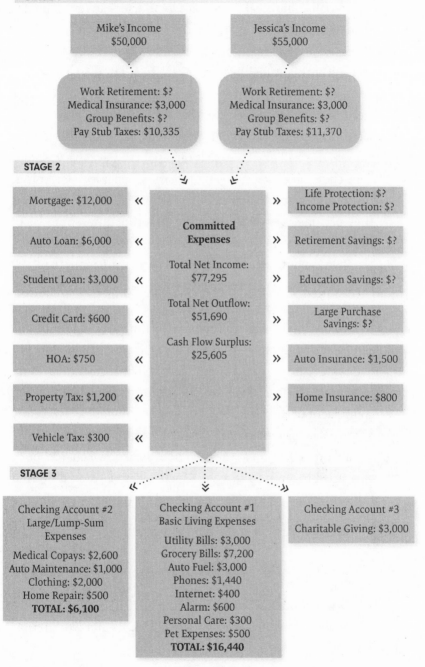

**STAGE 1**

Mike's Income
$50,000

Jessica's Income
$55,000

Work Retirement: $?
Medical Insurance: $3,000
Group Benefits: $?
Pay Stub Taxes: $10,335

Work Retirement: $?
Medical Insurance: $3,000
Group Benefits: $?
Pay Stub Taxes: $11,370

**STAGE 2**

Mortgage: $12,000 «

Auto Loan: $6,000 «

Student Loan: $3,000 «

Credit Card: $600 «

HOA: $750 «

Property Tax: $1,200 «

Vehicle Tax: $300 «

**Committed Expenses**

Total Net Income:
$77,295

Total Net Outflow:
$51,690

Cash Flow Surplus:
$25,605

» Life Protection: $?
Income Protection: $?

» Retirement Savings: $?

» Education Savings: $?

» Large Purchase Savings: $?

» Auto Insurance: $1,500

» Home Insurance: $800

**STAGE 3**

« ⋁ »

Checking Account #2
Large/Lump-Sum
Expenses

Medical Copays: $2,600
Auto Maintenance: $1,000
Clothing: $2,000
Home Repair: $500
**TOTAL: $6,100**

Checking Account #1
Basic Living Expenses

Utility Bills: $3,000
Grocery Bills: $7,200
Auto Fuel: $3,000
Phones: $1,440
Internet: $400
Alarm: $600
Personal Care: $300
Pet Expenses: $500
**TOTAL: $16,440**

Checking Account #3

Charitable Giving: $3,000

Initially, this breakdown may come across as very complex. Money appears to be going in all sorts of different directions. There are just too many arrows or, more specifically, too many steps. You might feel like this exercise is not worth the time or effort. I felt the same way the first time I logged onto Greg's website and viewed the extensive list of exercises there. There were so many different segments of my body that I needed to address. He had exercises that targeted the neck, back, shoulders, chest, abs, biceps, triceps, forearms, upper legs, lower legs, heart, and more. When examining the exercises, I saw that they became even more specific, targeting different areas of each muscle group. There were exercises for upper chest, lower chest, mid-chest, et cetera. In total, there were more than 690 different exercises for me to try to learn and apply.

Just seeing all of those exercises made me sick to my stomach. I asked myself if it was really worth the time to try and start this process. I already knew the basics, and shouldn't that be enough? I've come to learn that in both fitness and finance, the basics are never enough. To achieve success, we need to break down each component of what we are doing to make it work as efficiently as possible. But it does not have to all happen at once.

Take a look again at the cash flow breakdown chart. Notice that it is broken into three distinct stages, separated by bold horizontal lines. Likewise, you should create your own chart in three specific stages.

**Stage One**
1. Start by listing your gross income(s) in the top box(es).
2. Confirm what expenses are being systematically pulled out of your pay stubs to cover work benefits and work retire-

ment savings. (We will discuss how to adjust these benefits in chapter 5.)

3. Set up direct deposits of your income into one joint savings account. Call this account your "Committed Expenses" account. I suggest that you set up this account as a joint account because it shows that you put the family's cash flow needs and goals above your own. It also helps to avoid conflict when one family member makes more than the other. Remember, you are in this together!

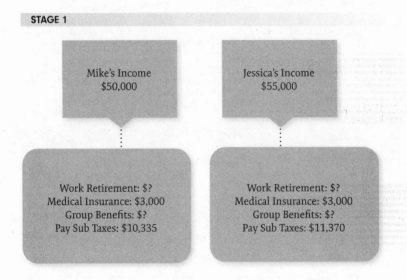

**STAGE 1**

Mike's Income
$50,000

Jessica's Income
$55,000

Work Retirement: $?
Medical Insurance: $3,000
Group Benefits: $?
Pay Sub Taxes: $10,335

Work Retirement: $?
Medical Insurance: $3,000
Group Benefits: $?
Pay Sub Taxes: $11,370

## Stage Two

4. Determine what committed expenses need to be pulled from this account. These expenses include liability payments, insurance policy premiums, and savings toward your long-term goals. Set up automatic withdrawals to have the pay-

ments made toward each of these items when due. These arrangements may be monthly, quarterly, semi-annually, or annually.

**STAGE 2**

Mortgage: $12,000 «

Auto Loan: $6,000 «

Student Loan: $3,000 «

Credit Card: $600 «

HOA: $750 «

Property Tax: $1,200 «

Vehicle Tax: $300 «

**Committed Expenses**

Total Net Income: $77,295

Total Net Outflow: $51,690

Cash Flow Surplus: $25,605

» Life Protection: $?
Income Protection: $?

» Retirement Savings: $?

» Education Savings: $?

» Large Purchase Savings: $?

» Auto Insurance: $1,500

» Home Insurance: $800

## Stage Three

5. Set up two (or three) checking accounts at a different banking institution. I strongly suggest that you use a unique bank for these accounts to help you separate your committed expenses and savings from your lump-sum and monthly living expenses. Label the three checking accounts as Large/Lump-Sum Expenses, Basic Living Expenses, and Charitable Giving (if you set up a third checking account).

6. Determine what primary and secondary committed expenses listed on your cash flow spreadsheet fall into each of these

categories. Divide these annual expenses into monthly expenses as needed, and authorize a systematic bank transfer into each of the accounts to cover the monthly expenses.

| Checking Account #2<br>Large / Lump-Sum Expenses | Checking Account #1<br>Basic Living Expenses | Checking Account #3<br>Charitable Giving: $3,000 |
| --- | --- | --- |
| Medical Copays: $2,600<br>Auto Maintenance: $1,000<br>Clothing: $2,000<br>Home Repair: $500<br>**TOTAL: $6,100** | Utility Bills: $3,000<br>Grocery Bills: $7,200<br>Auto Fuel: $3,000<br>Phones: $1,440<br>Internet: $400<br>Alarm: $600<br>Personal Care: $300<br>Pet Expenses: $500<br>**TOTAL: $16,440** | |

Once you have created a cash flow spreadsheet that identifies your committed and tax expenses, applying these expenses to the three stages should be a mostly straightforward process. In Stage One you do not need to set up any authorizations. Usually medical insurance, employee benefits, and taxes are automatically withdrawn from your pay stub. The employer does all the work for you. All that you need to do is direct your net income (after the deductions) into a joint "Committed Expenses" account. You will also want to confirm that you are paying the appropriate amount in taxes, which will be discussed in chapter 5.

Stage Two requires you to truly examine your cash flow spreadsheet and determine what expenses are primary committed. This process takes some time, but the result will be worth the effort. It forces you to determine what expenses you will continue to have regardless of your family's financial situation.

Many of these expenses remain fixed throughout the year, and some of them are bundled together. For example, if you own a home, it is likely that your monthly mortgage payment includes an escrow payment that covers your property taxes and home insurance premiums. By setting up systematic monthly payments from your Committed Expenses account into these various liabilities and expenses, you ensure that the bills are paid on time and that cash is available to cover the expenses.

In Stage Two you will also notice that there are several arrows pointing to boxes that represent your protection and long-term goals. In the sample annual cash flow statement, life and income protection needs are listed as well as retirement, education, and large-purchase savings. While we do not yet know the amounts needed in each of these categories, by placing them in Stage Two, Mike and Jessica are committing their incomes toward these priorities before advancing to Stage Three. They know that there is about $25,605 in surplus annual cash flow to dedicate toward these goals, as listed in the Committed Expenses box.

In Stage Three, establishing two or three separate checking accounts at a separate financial institution may seem like a huge and unnecessary hassle. I assure you that it is worth the effort. Having the accounts at the same location as your Committed Expenses account creates too much temptation and can blur the purpose of each account.

A fitness example illuminates this point. When I started doing Greg's workouts and came across an exercise that looked hard or that I had not tried before, I often would do another familiar exercise that might not have even fallen into the same muscle group. For example, I hated leg workouts. When instructed to do certain lunge, squat, or leg lift exercises, I would convince myself that going for a run or doing some sit-ups was a better use of my time. Sometimes I would even skip the entire leg workout and just move on to the next muscle group. I abandoned key muscle groups, and it did not take long before I could see the undesirable results of skipping steps and taking shortcuts. My upper body felt strong, but my lower body always felt weak. Only when I fully committed to Greg's program and instruction did I finally start to see the overall results.

This reality is as true in finance as it is in fitness. In fitness, you can have various goals: bigger biceps, leaner stomach, shredded shoulders, and a stronger heart. Each goal requires its own set of exercises and time commitment. In finance, your goals can include saving for retirement, protecting your family, preparing for college, building a cash reserve, and taking incredible vacations. Don't make it easy to take money from one category to cover the needs of another. For example, don't steal from your retirement funds to boost up your vacation spending.

Prevent the temptation by keeping the accounts used in Stage Two at a separate banking institution than the checking accounts used in Stage Three. While you can still transfer funds between the accounts in each stage, you are forced to make a conscious decision to sacrifice one goal for another. It becomes much harder to convince yourself that you can buy that new pair of shoes or golf clubs if the purchase requires you to pull from accounts dedicated to your children's education goals.

Stick to the cash flow breakdown. Confirm which expenses fall into each stage. Set up the automatic authorizations and don't skip steps. You will thank yourself later, and your family will thank you too!

## CHAPTER 4

# BE CERTAIN IN A WORLD OF UNCERTAINTY

*"Bet on yourself. If you bet on yourself, you'll never lose."*

**—GREG PLITT**

Greg always pushed himself to the limit, but he also knew the importance of not going into unfamiliar territory unprepared. With fitness, walking into a gym and jumping on a machine that you don't know how to use is asking for an injury. Fortunately, our bodies are usually very quick to tell us when we should stop or avoid certain activities. Pain is often felt instantaneously, and recovery usually takes only a short period of time.

The same is unfortunately not as true in finance. When a "what if" scenario comes up that we are not prepared to handle, the effects can be disastrous and often long lasting. The risks are also very difficult to identify and predict. We can never know for certain when a car is going to break down, when we will be in an accident, exactly how much college will cost in the next decade, or even how long we are going to live. There is a great deal of uncertainty in life, much of which could have a significant impact on your financial future and ability to achieve your goals.

This is especially true with families. As an individual, you get to limit the scope of your concerns to circumstances that could impact you directly. With families, everyone's circumstances play a pivotal role in impacting the overall family structure and family goals. Each member carries his or her own unique risks, and without accounting for all of the risks, one person's problem can quickly turn into a family emergency.

To use a fitness analogy, imagine a rowing team with four rowers. One rower gets a severe cramp and cannot row properly. Her paddle starts to drag on the water. The entire team is immediately impacted. They need to act fast to adjust to the situation. They can't throw her off; she's part of the team. They need a plan of action, and they need to be prepared *before* the race starts to be able to react as quickly as possible. If they wait and try to figure out what to do during the race, it will likely lead to confusion, anger, and possible further injury. It could also lead to the team not achieving its goal and finishing the race.

The same is true in finance. If a family takes the time to recognize and address the potential "what if" scenarios, its ability to recover quickly and stay on track with its goals improves dramatically! While every "what if" scenario cannot be addressed, there are several key steps that you can take to help prepare yourselves for financial uncertainties. The first is to know that there is always a cushion of cash available for emergency expenses.

## CASH RESERVES

*"The hardest things in life are done the least*
*but provide the most." —Greg Plitt*

A family's cash reserve often is one of the biggest psychological battles that couples encounter as they start the planning process. One spouse may want a significant reserve while the other does not see the purpose in having all that money just sitting idle. Both of their arguments are valid, but in the end, a reserve target needs to be set. The old rule of thumb was to have three to six months' worth of expenses. In more recent years, that threshold has changed to six to nine months' worth of expenses after taking into account the greater difficulty people have experienced finding new employment that fits their family living dynamic.

Savings equaling six to nine months' worth of living expenses sounds very reassuring, but there is little incentive to keep all that money sitting in a checking or savings account yielding a low rate of return. When money is available, it always seems to find a home. "Needs" inevitably arise, reducing the cash reserve below the target level.

The secret to building a cash reserve is that it must exist somewhere where you can't see it. The temptation of having cash that can easily be transferred from a savings into a checking account whenever needed is too high.

To put it in fitness terms, compare building a cash reserve to grocery shopping. You may have a set nutritional target for calories each day, but when you go to the grocery store, you buy enough food to last you the week or longer. You bring home all of that food and place it in your refrigerator and pantry.

Some food items require preparation before you can eat

them. Others are available to eat at your discretion. Think of the snack items that seem to always call your name as soon as you enter the kitchen: potato chips, string cheese, granola bars, pretzels, beer, et cetera. We all have our weaknesses. While there is nothing wrong with having snacks, comfort food that is easily available can quickly derail a diet goal and leave you wishing an hour later that you had made a better decision.

Even those with the greatest willpower struggle when temptation is placed directly in front of them. One of my favorite memories of Greg, a man who had an unbreakable iron will, was the evening of his sister Ginnie's wedding. We were all at the wedding reception, partying and dancing the night away. The Plitts know how to throw a great party, and this one was no exception. Alcohol and delicious food were abundant. As the evening drew to a close, I saw a figure hovering in the corner of the room. It was Greg, and he was all by himself, staring at a table wedged against the wall. His back was to me. As I approached, I could see that placed on top of the table was a tower of glazed donuts, set up like a castle of sugary delight. I had already eaten more than I could manage, yet seeing the donuts made my mouth water. I continued slowly inching toward Greg. He was hunched over, swaying slightly from side to side, staring intently at the table.

I was about to place my hand on his shoulder when he started mumbling to himself, "It's not . . . it's not . . . you know it's not worth it. You know it's not worth it." He was exhausted and inebriated. His willpower was at its weakest, and at that moment he made it perfectly clear that he, just like the rest of us, struggled with temptations that trick us into forgetting our goals and priorities, all for a quick jolt of short-term satisfaction.

I watched and waited. What would Greg do? Did he have it

in him to pull away when no one was there to encourage him to make the difficult choice? I wanted to speak, but my curiosity got the better of me. It felt like watching an Olympic sporting event. Fortunately for Greg, his sister called to him from the dance floor. He quickly left the table and made his way back to his friends. I never saw him eat a donut that night.

Greg's story reminds me of the difficulty of building and maintaining an accessible cash reserve. For many of us, if the reserves are large and readily available, that new pair of shoes or sleek new iPhone starts to look a whole lot more attractive. We convince ourselves that because we have the cash, it is fine to make use of it. We can always rebuild the reserves later.

This cycle of building and then splurging can become toxic. In fitness, it can lead to weight gain and poorer health. Imagine stocking your freezer with tubs of ice cream and your pantry with bags of chips. You rationalize that you'll buy the tempting food while it's on sale, but you'll eat it only when guests come over or you have a party. Every time you open the freezer or pantry, though, it calls your name, and you find yourself digging in on regular days. It would have been far safer to leave those items at the grocery store.

As you think of building up a cash reserve, recognize that temptation can quickly send your game plan off course. Also realize that temptation is more prevalent now than it has ever been before. Everything we want is easier to get.

We can walk into a grocery store and have aisles of candy bars, chips, and colas ready for the taking. At the office, vending machines are only a few steps away. Before we know it, drones may be dropping boxes of donuts on our front doorsteps. On the financial side, all we need to do is pull out our phones, click a few buttons, and money can leave our bank accounts in a matter of seconds. To make matters worse, we don't even need to have any money in the bank. Credit is available to just about anyone, even those who don't have the discipline to use it. We are bombarded by catchphrases that lure us into spending more than we intended: *Buy one, get the second 50 percent off... Available for a limited time only... It's your last chance... It's our going-out-of-business sale... Only a few left in stock—don't miss out!*

I go back to the phrase "Money not seen is money not missed." Don't give yourself the temptation. As explained in chapter 3, set up a Committed Expenses savings account at a bank separate from where you handle your everyday spending. Use your cash flow to determine what six months' worth of living expenses is and begin building your secondary reserve. For example, let's go back to Mike and Jessica's cash flow breakdown. See how the secondary cash reserve need has now been incorporated into Stage Two:

**STAGE 2**

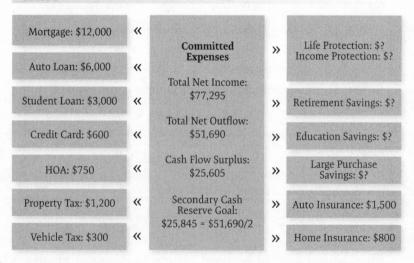

| Mortgage: $12,000 | « | **Committed Expenses** | » | Life Protection: $? Income Protection: $? |
|---|---|---|---|---|
| Auto Loan: $6,000 | « | Total Net Income: $77,295 | » | Retirement Savings: $? |
| Student Loan: $3,000 | « | Total Net Outflow: $51,690 | » | Education Savings: $? |
| Credit Card: $600 | « | Cash Flow Surplus: $25,605 | » | Large Purchase Savings: $? |
| HOA: $750 | « | Secondary Cash Reserve Goal: $25,845 = $51,690/2 | » | Auto Insurance: $1,500 |
| Property Tax: $1,200 | « | | » | Home Insurance: $800 |
| Vehicle Tax: $300 | « | | | |

Notice in the middle box in Stage Two that Mike and Jessica currently have a net annual outflow of $51,690. If their goal is to maintain a secondary cash reserve equal to six months of expenses, they will need to create a game plan to build up about $25,845 in their Committed Expenses account. Please note that other committed expenses like life and income protection have not yet been addressed. They will be discussed later in the chapter. When they are addressed, the cash reserve need will go up. Using this strategy, Mike and Jessica have the ability to identify what their cash reserve target should be and also keep the emergency reserve separate and not as easily accessible. Now all they need to do is work toward building their reserves to the target goal.

Some clients have asked when it might be appropriate to dip into a cash reserve. It is prudent to restrict withdrawals from committed reserves to only emergency expenses, such as unplanned surgery, your mortgage after a job loss, or a replacement car if yours dies unexpectedly. These expenses relate to necessities in your life: health, shelter, and transportation. They are not wants or luxuries. Consider a fitness analogy: If you sprain a muscle or your back gives out, you need to address the issue now before it gets worse, but if your headphones break or your workout clothes become outdated, you can still achieve a successful workout and postpone buying new equipment or clothing.

If you find yourself internally debating whether an expense counts as an emergency, it likely does not. Don't sabotage yourself!

## YOUR FAMILY, YOUR HEART: PROTECTING YOUR LIFE

*"When you help yourself, you feel good. But when you help somebody else, it's the greatest high in the world. It's addictive, it's contagious, and the world needs more of it." —Greg Plitt*

As you work to build up your cash reserve, you need to recognize that your (and your spouse's) ability to earn an income and care for your family has an incredible value. It is what you might refer to as your "human life value." While it is impossible to give a value to everything that you and your spouse do for your family, denying that your family would suffer if something were to happen to either of you is, simply put, a selfish act. You together are the beating heart of the family, and without one of you, the heart cannot as efficiently pump the necessary nutrients to keep the family functioning.

For many of us, it's not so much that we deny our value to our family. It's more that we ignore it. We convince ourselves, especially during our younger years, that we are invincible and that we cannot die. We tell ourselves that we'll worry about the "what ifs" of life and death when the need arises. We'll wait until after we are married, have kids, purchase our first home, et cetera. The harsh truth is that waiting can have very expensive consequences.

Many people fail in life financially not because of small financial mistakes. They fail because circumstances arise that are beyond their control, and they are not prepared. Death is certainly something that is beyond our control. Yes, we can strive to stay healthy, eat well, and exercise, and those efforts likely will prolong our lives, but some life events are unavoidable.

Here I will share with you a personal story. I started as a financial advisor right out of college, at age 22. I was dating a woman named Laura, whom I had met during our sophomore year at the University of Richmond. My new job pulled me back to Maryland, while Laura was moving on to graduate school at the University of North Carolina at Chapel Hill. We intended to keep the relationship going as long as possible, and I found myself traveling down to Chapel Hill on weekends at least once a month.

Eventually, we ended up renting an apartment together as I expanded my practice to include clients in both Maryland and North Carolina. We knew we wanted to get married, buy a home, have one or two children, and see where the future would take us. No goals seemed very concrete at the time. We were new to adulthood and were just trying to figure it all out.

When starting as a financial planner, I was told by my peers that it was ill advised to recommend a product or strategy that I would not use myself. I didn't think much of it at the time, but one product I recommended to clients was life insurance. It was fairly easy to determine a client's life protection needs. I would identify what liabilities they would need to pay off, estimate how much net income they would potentially generate between now and when they wanted to retire, and take into account any education goals for their children. I would determine the total life protection need and then discuss options for how best to address it.

For Laura and me, these were all still unknowns. We didn't own a home, were not yet married, and had no children. All that I could do was sit down with Laura and together try to make some sense of what we wanted for our futures and what needs we would likely want to protect. In the end, we determined our basic goals and purchased 20-year term life policies with the hope that our goals would one day become realities. We selected 20-year terms because we intended to have children in the near future and wanted policies that would cover us during their dependent years, up until college age.

Fast forward about eight years. We were married, owned our first home with a fixed mortgage, had a daughter, and were expecting our second child in five months. Life was moving quickly. Laura had stopped working to dedicate more time to raising our children. I was working full time and spending my free time running triathlons, taking bike rides, and enjoying other outdoor activities with my family. I was in pretty good shape. One day, I finished a run and got ready to take a shower. As I removed my shirt, I noticed an odd-looking rash on my stomach. It didn't hurt, so I didn't think much of it. I figured it was probably just heat rash and would go away soon.

But the rash did not go away. It was still there a week later. I went to the dermatologist to get it checked out, and, after a few tests, they determined that it was the result of lymphoma. All of a sudden, my simple life became a lot more complicated with a lot more questions. I had just turned 30. Before I knew it, we were scheduling appointments with specialists and I was set to have a full internal body scan as well as a bone marrow biopsy. My mortality started to feel much more real.

After all the tests, I was given the good news that I would not need to begin chemotherapy or start taking any medications. It appeared that the lymphoma impacted only my skin and that the small rashes would just come and go. My wife and I were very excited by the wonderful news, but my mind started to reflect on those term life policies we had purchased. The next day when I went into the office, I called the underwriter for my term life policy and asked him what rating a person with my condition would receive if he were applying for a new life insurance policy. The underwriter told me that it was very likely that the application would be rejected immediately.

As I hung up the phone, I realized that the term life policy I had purchased for myself years ago, before Laura and I were married, would not even be an option had I waited. I got the policy when I was young and healthy. I purchased enough coverage to make sure that my wife and potential children would be fine if something ever happened to me. Now I had a policy that could not be cancelled by the insurer, with a healthy preferred rating premium that could not be changed. To make things even better, the policy had an "extended conversion period" rider that allowed me at any point during the policy's term to change it from a term to a permanent policy at the same health rating.

So what is the takeaway from this story? Waiting to protect your life until after you have committed yourself to a mortgage, a spouse, a family, or any other major obligations is like playing a game of Russian roulette, except this time it is the people who depend on you who are going to get hurt. The fortunate news is that applying for life insurance is a fairly easy and painless process.

Some clients ask if it is better to increase their group life coverage benefit or to purchase an individual term or a permanent life policy. I almost always prefer individual life coverage over increased group life coverage. The primary rationale is control. You do not own your group life coverage. It is a benefit made available to you through your employer. If you leave the employer, the protection benefit also often ends. Imagine starting a new job and applying for a high level of group life coverage when you are still young and healthy. Now 10 years have passed and you wish to change jobs, but your health has declined. Your new employer does not offer any group life coverage. You may be forced to decide between staying with a job that you no longer enjoy or leaving the job and putting your family's security at risk if something were ever to happen to you. Individual life coverage is yours. You own the policy. It goes with you no matter where you go. You remain in control.

When you are ready to look into options on how to best protect your family in the event of a death, here are a few other key points to consider:

- Life insurance is almost always less expensive for women than it is for men, assuming the same health and age.

- Most companies offer breakpoints in life coverage, meaning that the cost per thousand dollars of coverage goes down if you acquire a certain level of coverage. These breakpoints often exist at $250,000 and $1,000,000 in coverage. This means that if you decide to get a policy with a $200,000 death benefit, you may find that the $250,000 coverage is extremely close in price.

- With many companies, paying the premium annually can reduce the total cost of insurance.

- Many companies allow you to pay with a credit card if you want to collect points or get cash back.

- When looking at term life coverage, ask if the policy has an "extended conversion period" rider. As mentioned earlier, this rider allows you to change your policy from a term to a permanent policy at any point during the life of the policy at your original health rating.

- When researching providers, make sure to look at each one's Comdex ranking. This is a composite score (on a scale of 1 to 100) of evaluations from major insurance rating organizations, including A.M. Best, Fitch, Moody's, and S&P. An insurance company must have ratings from at least two insurance rating organizations to have a Comdex ranking. Consider looking for companies with a Comdex ranking of at least 90.

- Many articles highlight both the benefits and drawbacks of permanent life coverage versus term life coverage. Term life policies usually have periods of 10, 15, 20, or 30 years. Permanent life policies last a lifetime as long as the cost of insurance is paid. These policies come in different forms: whole life, universal life, variable universal life, and more. My suggestion is to address your protection needs initially with term life policies and then examine the permanent life policy options once all comprehensive planning goals and needs are on track. The monthly premiums for permanent life policies are almost always significantly higher than for term life policies.

- Don't feel that you need to do all of the work yourselves. Contact two or three life insurance providers and ask them to help you determine what level of coverage you need. Ask what method they will use to calculate your need, and see which method makes the most sense to you. (Review chapter 10 to determine who would best help you address your life protection needs.)

- If possible, apply for the coverage with your spouse; then you can hold one another accountable in making sure that you each complete the medical interview and other required steps to obtain coverage.

## YOUR INCOME, YOUR BLOOD:
## PROTECTING AGAINST DISABILITY

*"Walk through the mud in life if you ever want
to get to the higher ground."* —Greg Plitt

Addressing your life protection need is an essential to-do when it comes to helping secure your family's financial future. Just as essential is addressing your income protection need. Your heart is responsible for pumping blood throughout the body, but it is your blood that brings oxygen and nutrients where they are needed.

You can imagine very clearly how your death would impact your spouse and children. Imagining a disability and its impact on the family is much more difficult. There are so many different possibilities, some minor and easy to adjust to, some catastrophic. Your inability to do your job could easily result from something as simple as a sprained wrist to something as complicated as a metastasized brain tumor.

There are things that you can do to help prevent or reduce the likelihood of experiencing a disability. You can exercise, eat well, and avoid risky activities like base jumping and skydiving, but your ability to control what happens to your body is limited. You can't always control car accidents, sports injuries, or biological abnormalities. You can try to avoid activities that involve certain levels of risk, but avoiding all forms of risk is impossible.

Even if you are not a risk-taker, your job likely requires you to drive or bike to work. Your job also could require you to sit at your desk for an extended period of time, which can lead to health problems down the road. Some disabilities are instantaneous and obvious, while others can creep up on you. Preparing for income loss scenarios is the next step in helping to ensure that your family's goals don't get derailed. Here is where you have three options.

## Option One: Reduce Your Standard of Living

The first option is to determine how your disability would impact your family and whether they could handle a reduced standard of living. Most employers offer some level of group disability coverage, usually equal to about 50 percent to 60 percent of your income. Could your family survive if your income was slashed in half? Some individuals would say yes, and they probably could make it work. But the more important question is whether you would be able to stay on track to still achieve your family's future goals like college education and retirement.

Another important factor to consider is that group disability coverage usually covers only the employee's *base* income. This means that any bonus income or employer-provided benefits, like an employer's match into a work retirement plan, would not be covered. Using the cash flow example for Mike and Jessica, Mike's $5,000 bonus income would not be covered. If his employer offered a 3 percent match on his 401(k) plan, it also would not be covered. The impact of the disability and the minimal level of group disability coverage can be far more impactful than most individuals realize!

## Option Two: Build a Strong Short-Term Reserve

If you do not want to reduce your standard of living, your second option is to build a very robust cash reserve and hope that your disability is a short-term situation. Having a large cash reserve can help to cover unexpected medical bills and give some cushion in case your income is reduced for a few months.

## Option Three: Transfer the Risk

While the first and second options offer some level of protection and planning for a short-term disability, they don't address the "what if" scenario of a long-term disability. What happens if the issue persists or gets worse? Health insurance may help with some of the medical bills, but what about all of the other commitments you have to your family and their future? The third option is to transfer the risk or, put more bluntly, to purchase gap individual income protection (disability coverage). This coverage is meant to supplement your employer-provided group benefit. See the following disability (DI) income chart example for Mike.

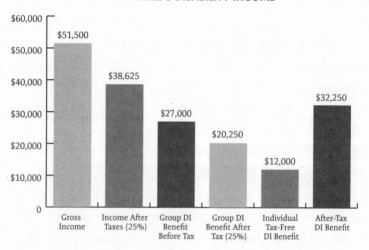

**MIKE'S DISABILITY INCOME**

Mike has a base income of $45,000 plus a $5,000 annual bonus. He also receives a 3 percent match on his 401(k) plan, which equals $1,500 of additional compensation each year for a total of $51,500 (see column 1). If we assume that 25 percent of his income goes toward taxes, Mike then has a net income of $38,625 annually (see column 2).

Mike's employer offers a group disability benefit of 60 percent of his base income, or $27,000 (see column 3). Because the employer pays for this benefit, the disability income is taxed as ordinary income before it is paid out to Mike. If we assume the same 25 percent is withheld for taxes on Mike's disability income, his net disability income will be $20,250 (see column 4). This means that if Mike experiences a disability, his net income will go from $38,625 (column 2) down to $20,250 (column 4). The total drop in net income would be $18,375. Mike and Jessica may be able to survive this magnitude of drop, but the funds that they could dedicate toward their future goals would be diminished drastically.

To help reduce the impact of the disability, Mike purchases an individual gap disability policy that provides a $1,000 monthly benefit or $12,000 annually (see column 5). Because Mike pays for the policy with money in his Committed Expenses account that has already been taxed, the individual disability income benefit comes to him tax free. Adding this tax-free income to Mike's group disability benefit increases his total disability coverage benefit to $32,250 (see column 6).

Mike and Jessica determine that a net income drop of $6,375 would be much easier for their family to handle than a drop of $18,375. They also know that they can afford the coverage using money from their cash flow surplus. The "what if" of Mike becoming too sick or hurt to go to work is no longer as severe, and their minds are at ease.

They both decide to address their life and income protection needs. After meeting with several insurance agents, they choose one and each purchase a $1 million 20-year term life policy to protect their family. The annual premium for Mike's life policy is $525, and the annual premium for Jessica's life policy is $450. They also decide to each purchase gap individual long-term disability policies to supplement their group long-term disability coverage. The annual premium for Mike's disability policy is $1,650, and the annual premium for Jessica's disability policy is $1,850. They update their cash flow statement as well as their cash flow breakdown chart to show the following:

**STAGE 2**

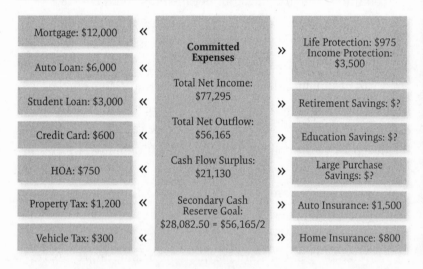

| Committed Expenses Inputs | Committed Expenses | Planned Outflow |
|---|---|---|
| Mortgage: $12,000 « | | » Life Protection: $975 Income Protection: $3,500 |
| Auto Loan: $6,000 « | Total Net Income: $77,295 | |
| Student Loan: $3,000 « | | » Retirement Savings: $? |
| Credit Card: $600 « | Total Net Outflow: $56,165 | » Education Savings: $? |
| HOA: $750 « | Cash Flow Surplus: $21,130 | » Large Purchase Savings: $? |
| Property Tax: $1,200 « | Secondary Cash Reserve Goal: $28,082.50 = $56,165/2 | » Auto Insurance: $1,500 |
| Vehicle Tax: $300 « | | » Home Insurance: $800 |

Notice that the total net outflow in the Committed Expenses section has increased, as has the secondary cash reserve goal. Make sure to update your cash flow breakdown with every cash flow change that you make.

When you are ready to look into options on how to best protect your family in the event of a disability, here are a few key points to consider:

- Disability insurance is almost always less expensive for men than it is for women, assuming the same health and age. This is the opposite of life coverage.

- Similar to term life coverage, paying premiums annually often can reduce the total cost of insurance.

- Similar to term life coverage, you often can pay the premium with a credit card if you want to collect points or miles.

- Your elimination period is the period of time you have to wait before the benefit begins. Try selecting a waiting period that lines up with your total months of cash reserve. For example, if your goal is to have six months of living expenses, then you should select a 180-day elimination period.

- Many policies offer an assortment of riders, which are add-ons to the policy. Consider riders that offer a cost-of-living adjustment (COLA) benefit as well as a future purchase option (FPO) benefit. These riders allow your disability income benefit to grow without proof of insurability both before and during a period of disability.

- As with life coverage, don't feel that you need to do all of the work yourselves. The same agents who help you with life coverage also may be able to help with disability coverage.

- Ask your employer whether the company that handles the group disability coverage offers any discounts for individuals who wish to purchase additional gap individual coverage. You can also determine whether supplemental coverage is available through the employer. If so, consider taking full advantage of the additional group supplemental coverage.

## YOUR WISHES, YOUR LEGACY: ESTATE PLANNING

*"You only live once, but if you do it right,*
*once is enough." —Mae West*

Once your life and income protection needs are addressed, it is time to move on to the most important part of protection planning: your estate and your legacy. For many individuals, the word *estate* means the stuff that we leave behind when we die. We often think of estate planning as something done only by rich people who have buckets of money and want to pass it on to their children and grandchildren. In reality, estate planning is just as critical for the 20-something first-time parent as it is for the retiree approaching his or her later years of life. Estate planning has very little to do with your assets. It has a whole lot more to do with your wishes and dreams.

I am going to tell you another story about my cousin Greg, but this is not one of praise. Rarely in my life did I see my cousin fail. He was committed. He was strategic. He loved his parents, his sister, his brother-in-law, and his nephews. All of the cousins knew that one of Greg's personal missions in life was to take care of his family in whatever manner necessary. His love for his family was unquestionable. While he did not have a wife and children, there were so many people who depended on him. He had hundreds of thousands of fans, his family, his dogs, and the employees who worked on his website. He also had a very serious girlfriend he hoped to one day marry.

Soon after Greg's death, my parents, my sister, and I joined the Plitt family at Greg's house in California. Other family members also had arrived to offer their support. We were all crippled emotionally, and we were looking for answers. None of us had expected Greg to die. We started to ask, "What were his wishes? Did he have a place where he wanted to be buried? Should we cremate his body? What about his dogs or the employees with his company?" No one knew exactly where to start.

We gathered in the living room to try to figure out what to do next. Someone asked if Greg had a will. None of us knew the answer. We started searching the house, scrambling through stacks of papers, inspecting any possible location where Greg might have hidden some type of document describing his wishes. We found nothing. It was now up to the family to try to figure out what Greg might have wanted. Fortunately, they were able to work together and did an incredible job. Greg would have been proud.

After the funeral, I learned more about the difficulties that Greg's family had to endure. There were accounts that needed to be closed, salaries that needed to be paid, dogs who needed a new home, websites that needed to be updated, a mortgage that needed to be paid . . . this list went on and on. Greg's father, who lived in Florida, was forced to spend weeks in California to meet with attorneys working to get his son's affairs in order. I can only imagine the toll it took on his mind and body. It took several months of hard work and frequent travel before Greg's father was able to return home for good.

I share this story with you because it highlights the immense impact we have on the lives of those around us. The impact only compounds as we bring others into our lives though marriage and having children. Estate planning is the process of helping those who care for you and depend on you to understand your wishes both before and after death.

## Basic Will

So what could Greg have done to make such a difficult experience for his family a little less chaotic? Greg could have created a basic will. A basic will provides guidance on what you would like to have happen in the event of your death. It allows you to select an executor, the person or organization that you wish to be in charge of handling matters related to your death. The will gives you the ability to give general or specific instructions as to funeral arrangements, distribution of your assets, and other personal matters. For families with children, one of the most essential functions of a will is the selection of a guardian.

## The Guardian

The guardian is the person or people you select to care for your children in the event that both parents pass away. Usually, couples name their spouse as the primary guardian, but selecting the person who will care for the children if both spouses pass away is often a very challenging exercise. Still, it is one that must be done! Otherwise, it is up to the state to select the guardian, and that person may be the last person that either spouse would have selected.

Because this decision is so difficult, it often becomes a discussion topic that many spouses put on the back burner. They tell themselves that it is incredibly unlikely that both of them will die while the children are young, and statistically they are right. What happens, though, when they decide to take their first trip together without the kids? What if something happens on the flight or while visiting some unfamiliar location?

My sister, Kathy, had just these thoughts before a mini-vacation to Las Vegas with her husband, Matt. They are parents to three wonderful young children, and they both work full time. They understood why setting up a will was important, but they had yet to do it—what would happen after their deaths and who would care for their children were decisions that seemed too difficult to tackle.

As the flight date approached, Kathy started to grow concerned. She hated flying, and the idea of something happening to both her and Matt terrified her. In a panic, she called me two days prior to their trip to ask what they needed to do to protect their children in the event that her fears were realized. Fortunately, she and Matt both had already acquired enough life insurance to cover the kids financially, but the guardian question loomed large.

Kathy and Matt both come from big, loving families, which made their decision even more critical. If something did happen, would their parents and siblings and cousins and friends all be able to agree on who would be best to take on the role of guardian? Might that person be too young or too old to handle the responsibility? Would there be enough room in the guardian's home? Would the children have to move to different schools or to a different state? Could the guardian handle the financial responsibility? Only Kathy and Matt could fully answer these questions and select the person or couple they felt would be the most appropriate fit.

Kathy was pleased to discover that basic estate documents can be created very quickly. Using an online site dedicated to generating legal documents, they created basic wills, health care directives, and power of attorney documents. They identified their executors and their guardians. They had the documents printed off, signed, notarized, and witnessed all before they arrived at the airport. That morning Kathy awoke relieved, knowing that should something go wrong, her children would be in good hands and her family would know what to do.

## Revocable Trust

While I was incredibly happy that my sister and brother-in-law had addressed their basic estate planning needs, they had one critical task to address upon their return from Las Vegas: establishing a revocable trust. I suggest this to all families with children. According to *Webster's Dictionary*, a trust is a "fiduciary relationship in which one party holds legal title to another's property for the benefit of a party who holds equitable title to the property." Simply put, a trust is a vehicle that can hold the assets in a person's estate once that person has passed away. This could include real estate, cars, investment accounts, and cash from processed life insurance policies. The revocable trust can be established either under a will or as a separate estate document.

The importance of a trust is related to two numbers: 18 and 21. I explained to Kathy and Matt that if no trust is set up, once their children reach one of those ages (depending on the state), all estate assets that are dedicated to the children will then be under the children's control. The guardian is no longer in charge.

At ages 18 and 21, most of us have little to no idea of how to handle large sums of money. Try to think of how responsible you were at 18. Now imagine that you, at that age, have just received full ownership of an estate that includes a lump sum of cash from two life insurance policies, a home that you will co-own with your siblings, and assets left to you by your parents.

Would your 18-year-old self make the most prudent choices with all of that money? Would you set aside a large portion of those funds for a new home or college expenses or a future family or other longer-term retirement goals? The simple truth is that we don't know, but a trust gives parents the ability to maintain control over those assets even in death. It allows them to decide when and how their children will receive their inheritances if something should happen to both parents.

It also allows them to assign a specific person known as the trustee, who is given the responsibility of managing the assets inside of the trust until the assets are set to be passed on to the beneficiaries. The trustee does not have to be the same person as the guardian. For example, you may feel that one family member is more appropriate to care for your children in the event of your death, but another family member is more financially savvy or financially responsible.

### Health Care Directive/Power of Attorney

In addition to preparing for post-death scenarios, we also need to recognize that unforeseen events in life can impact not only ourselves but those around us. For example, imagine that a husband is in a car accident. He has a well-funded cash reserve and has also addressed his income protection needs. But now he is in the hospital and the doctor is asking his wife if she has approval to make health care decisions for her husband. The bank is also calling her, telling her that the money she needs to cover the medical bills cannot be withdrawn because her name is not listed on the savings account.

She is an emotional wreck, and now she is discovering that she has no authority to make the critical decisions necessary to help her husband recover. To make matters worse, her mother-in-law has arrived at the hospital, and they disagree on what next steps the doctors should take. The family is in a state of complete disarray, anger, and confusion.

These complications could have been avoided if the husband had created just two basic estate planning documents: a health care directive and a power of attorney. The health care directive, also known as a living will, is "a legal document in which a person expresses his or her wishes regarding medical treatment in the event of incapacity" (*Webster's*). Simply put, it gives doctors and family members direction on your wishes as they relate to discontinuance of life support.

The power of attorney is a document that gives someone "the right to act and make decisions for another person in business and legal matters" (*Learner's Dictionary*). Power of attorney authorizations can be general and apply to any scenario or they can be restricted to certain decision areas, like medical care or financial management. A health care power of attorney, for example, is a document through which a person appoints a health care agent or surrogate to make other (not end-of-life) health care decisions for that person.

Had the husband created these documents, his wife would not have been burdened with trying to determine what directions to give the doctors. She would not have had to argue with her mother-in-law over what he would have wanted. She would have had the authority to act in her husband's place and gain access to the cash in his savings account to cover the unexpected medical bills. These estate planning documents would have simplified the process and helped avoid unnecessary stress for everyone involved.

The key to the will, the trust, and all of the other estate planning documents is that they give families control and peace of mind in knowing that their wishes are clear and can be followed. When you are ready to address your estate planning needs, here are a few key points to consider:

- Do it right the first time. If you try an online site and find that you are having difficulty answering the questions or understanding the language, don't move forward with the site. Instead, consult an estate attorney. While the cost may be higher, soliciting expert advice will give you greater peace of mind and ensure that you have the necessary estate documents to protect your family.

- Make sure to ask your estate attorney to provide you with a list of beneficiary recommendations for your investment accounts and insurance policies. One of the biggest mistakes I repeatedly have seen clients make is creating all their estate documents and then forgetting to update their beneficiary designations. In estate planning, the beneficiary designations listed on your accounts and insurance policies override what your will or trust documents instruct. For example, many people list on their insurance policies and investment account that their spouses are their primary beneficiaries and their children are their secondary beneficiaries in equal shares. If you create a revocable trust that is meant to hold the assets in the event of your and your spouse's death, but you do not update the secondary beneficiary designations, those estate assets will likely skip going into the trust and will instead go straight to the children. This leaves the newly established trust without value or purpose.

- Make sure to provide the executor, the guardian, and the trustee with a copy of your estate documents. Also let them know where the originals are held.

- Create a document that lists all of your user names and passwords to your various accounts and social media platforms. Keep this document in a secure location with your original estate documents. Make sure to update the document as you change user names and passwords.

- Review your estate documents every five to seven years to confirm that all are still in good order and that no changes need to be made.

## CHAPTER 5

# EATING YOUR TAXES, PAYING YOUR CALORIES

*"Opportunities don't come knocking on the door. They present themselves when you knock the door down."*

**—GREG PLITT**

My cousin Greg loved helping people achieve physical success. He made exercise exciting, but one challenge that seemed to come up again and again from the members posting on his site involved working out and not seeing immediate results. Members would state that they were pushing it in the gym, but the weight was not coming off. Greg would dive a bit deeper and discover that the workout was not the issue. It was the diet. We somehow convince ourselves that when we start working out more, that is an excuse to start eating more. Our goal may be to lose weight, but we sabotage it every time we eat that dessert, choose soda over water, or go back to the kitchen for that second serving of food.

Our bodies require food. Trying to starve ourselves and also achieve a consistent, productive workout is impossible. Calories are the fuel that keeps our bodies moving. The protein creates the muscle. We need a certain daily intake of calories to stay healthy and survive. The problem is that society makes it nearly impossible to stick to a healthy eating program. Social norms often tell us that hanging out with friends can only be done with food or alcohol involved. When we go to the grocery store, aisles of processed carbohydrates sit waiting for us. It is not until we figure out how to restrict our daily calories to the necessary amount required that we truly begin to see the results.

This same logic applies to taxes in the world of finance. We all need to pay taxes. Taxes go toward our schools, our police, our military, our roads, and a multitude of other priorities that make our society function. Paying too much in taxes every year, however, limits our ability to achieve our personal goals. While the government is meant to help you achieve a certain quality of life, it is not the government's responsibility to ensure your family's happiness or security. That responsibility falls on you and your spouse. Paying more in taxes than you need to is a guaranteed way to slow down your progress and diminish your results. The worst part is that, unlike eating a carb-loaded dessert, you get no immediate satisfaction from paying too much in taxes.

Taxes, like calories, are often unseen. With calories, you don't realize how much you are eating until you step on the scale or look in the mirror. With taxes, you don't realize how much you are paying until you file your tax returns at the end of each year. Many individuals have no idea how much they are paying in taxes or how much they should be paying. It should not surprise you that most of the wealthiest individuals on the planet are masters at working the tax system.

Greg was a master as much outside of the gym as he was inside. His eating patterns were consistent. Over the years, he studied his body to determine what supplements worked best, when to consume certain types of food, and which foods provided the greatest nutritional value. To be fair, he was still human. He occasionally enjoyed a pizza or a burger or a slice of carrot cake, but he made sure to stick to his program as consistently as possible. He knew that the fuel that made his body function was as critical to his success as the way he put that fuel to work in the gym.

In finance, your income is that fuel. We need income to survive. We need it to pay for food, shelter, and every other committed expense we have listed on our cash flow spreadsheets. Taxes, while important, should be viewed as the waste. Taxes are the excess fat that slows you down. Finding strategies to minimize that lost income can very quickly yield motivating results.

To understand how to limit taxes, you first need to understand how taxes work. We do not live in a flat-tax society. Based on the government's current tax structure, the more you make within certain income thresholds, the higher the government's cut becomes. In 2018, the federal income tax brackets for a married couple filing jointly were as follows:

| TAX RATE | INCOME RANGE |
|---|---|
| 10% | $0 to $19,050 |
| 12% | $19,051 to $77,400 |
| 22% | $77,401 to $165,000 |
| 24% | $165,001 to $315,000 |
| 32% | $315,001 to $400,000 |
| 35% | $400,001 to $600,000 |
| 37% | $600,001 + |

This means that if your family makes a combined household taxable income of $80,000, the first $19,050 will be taxed at 10 percent. The income above $19,050 will be taxed at 12 percent until you get to $77,400. Only the remaining $2,600 in income will fall into the 22 percent federal tax bracket. It is very important to understand that only the income that falls in the income range will be taxed at the higher rate. See the following tax bracket example chart:

## TAX BRACKET EXAMPLE

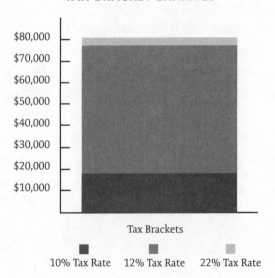

It is also important to understand that the tax is calculated based on your family's *taxable* income. To determine that number, start by looking at your previous year's tax statement or contacting your tax advisor. Study your tax statement to determine what deductions and exemptions you are able to use to reduce your taxable income. Walk through the statement with your tax advisor.

Once you know your estimated taxable income, the next step is to determine whether you want to:

1. Defer paying taxes now so that you can pay them later
2. Pay the taxes now and have the rest of your money grow tax-free
3. Pay the taxes now and be required to pay them every year on any growth you may have

The third option does not sound all that attractive, but it is the option that most Americans take. Most Americans don't look into what strategies are available when it comes to reducing taxes. They simply take their paycheck as soon as they receive it and stash the cash in their checking account.

It's almost like walking into your kitchen, opening the refrigerator, and seeing tuna fish, an apple, and a slice of chocolate cake. You know the tuna fish and apple are the healthier choices, but the cake seems to call you. It looks so good just sitting on your plate. You know that it will give you that short burst of energy and satisfaction, but the energy will be fleeting, and you will be left having to absorb all that excess caloric waste.

It's hard to see how much of that cake is going to end up becoming waste. All those calories are hidden under layers of chocolate frosting. The same is true of your paycheck. If you are a W-2 employee, your taxes come out automatically.

You may not even notice them. All you see is the checking account jumping up for the month, and it feels good. You even get excited when the IRS gives you a tax refund, viewing it as some sort of gift from the government. To be clear, it is no gift! It is *your* money. It is the money that you could have used during the year to work toward your long-term goals. It is essentially an interest-free loan that you gave to the government.

If you want to get a sense of how frustrating it can be to see what you are actually paying in taxes, ask someone who is self-employed. Many small business owners have to pay their taxes on a quarterly basis. They have to save up the money every three months and make sure the tax payments are made on time. If they don't, penalties are applied.

Look at your previous year's tax statements to determine how much money was deducted for federal and state taxes. The purpose of the exercise is to let you know your starting point. Once you know your taxable income and your total taxes paid, you then get to make a key decision. Do you think you should pay less in taxes now with the hope that your taxes will be lower in the future, or pay the taxes owed now and allow a portion of your savings to grow tax-free?

It needs to be understood that we have no idea what taxes will look like in the future. All of the tax brackets could certainly go up, but the more likely scenario is that they will go up for individuals and families whose taxable incomes fall into the highest income brackets. As many politicians say, "That is where the money is." Given this understanding, you can view the 12 percent and 22 percent federal brackets as the two differentiator brackets. It is very unlikely that you will pay less than 10 percent or 12 percent in federal taxes in retirement. It is also very possible that you will be able to avoid the 22 percent federal bracket in retirement. The objective is to give your family options. One of the best ways to determine these options is to use a strategy called the Tax Control Triangle:

## TAX CONTROL TRIANGLE

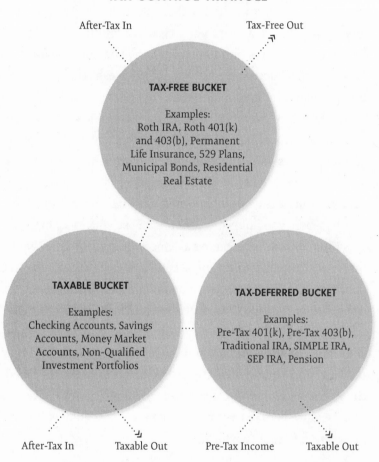

After-Tax In                                  Tax-Free Out

**TAX-FREE BUCKET**

Examples:
Roth IRA, Roth 401(k)
and 403(b), Permanent
Life Insurance, 529 Plans,
Municipal Bonds, Residential
Real Estate

**TAXABLE BUCKET**

Examples:
Checking Accounts, Savings
Accounts, Money Market
Accounts, Non-Qualified
Investment Portfolios

**TAX-DEFERRED BUCKET**

Examples:
Pre-Tax 401(k), Pre-Tax 403(b),
Traditional IRA, SIMPLE IRA,
SEP IRA, Pension

After-Tax In    Taxable Out    Pre-Tax Income    Taxable Out

## TAXABLE BUCKET

There are three separate buckets inside the triangle. The first is your taxable bucket. Money that goes into this bucket has already been taxed. It is the net income that you receive on your pay stub. Once this money is invested, its growth is taxable, meaning that any interest or dividends or recognized gains that the money receives is taxed every year, often at the family's highest tax bracket. Savings vehicles that fall into this bucket include checking, savings, and money market accounts, as well as CDs, stocks, bonds, mutual funds, and other investments that are held in "non-qualified" accounts. "Non-qualified" means that the accounts do not qualify for any tax benefits.

So why would anyone want to have a non-qualified account? The simple answer is my favorite *F* word: *flexibility*. Non-qualified accounts offer significant flexibility. You can add to them and make withdrawals from them at your discretion, usually without fear of tax penalties. These savings vehicles are your liquid reserves and should also be where you hold your primary and secondary cash reserves.

While it may feel good to have more than six months' worth of reserves sitting in a checking account, like the example with the chocolate cake, it is wasted calories, or more specifically, wasted opportunity. The likelihood of your needing six months' worth of reserves all at once is extraordinarily low. That cash may sit there for years, yielding a minimal return (possibly less than 1 percent) and having the little interest that it generates taxed by the government every year. So while it is important to have a cash reserve, once your reserve needs are met, you then need to choose between the other two buckets.

## TAX-DEFERRED BUCKET

The second bucket is your tax-deferred bucket. Money goes into this bucket pre-tax, meaning that it is not currently taxed. For example, if your family made $80,000 in taxable income in 2018 and you contributed $2,600 to this bucket, you would reduce your taxable income to $77,400 and avoid paying any federal income tax at 22 percent. This is the bucket you would use if you think that your taxable income will be lower in retirement than it is today. If you have income that currently is being taxed at 22 percent or higher, pre-tax retirement savings is the way to go!

Savings vehicles that fall into this pre-tax bucket include traditional work retirement plans (e.g., traditional 401(k), 403(b), 457(b), profit sharing, SIMPLE IRAs, SEP IRAs) and traditional IRAs. Pensions and Social Security also fall into this category. It is important to understand that certain types of pensions as well as Social Security are considered *defined-benefit* plans. These plans are based on formulas, and you as an employee have no choice as to how much is contributed to these plans.

The other type of retirement plan is called a *defined-contribution* plan. These plans give you a choice. You can choose not to fund them at all, or you can allocate up to a certain amount of your income to the plans each year. In 2018, 401(k)s and 403(b)s have maximum annual pre-tax or Roth contribution limits of $18,500, or $24,500 if you are over the age of 50. This additional contribution bump is called a "catch-up" contribution. Other plans have different maximum thresholds as listed below:

| PLAN | MAXIMUM ANNUAL CONTRIBUTION FOR 2018 |
|------|--------------------------------------|
| Traditional IRA | $5,500, or $6,500 if over age 50 |
| SIMPLE IRA | $12,500, or $15,500 if over age 50 |
| SEP IRA | Lesser of 25% of your income or $55,000 |
| 457(b) Plan | $18,500 |

To give employees an incentive to participate in these plans, employers often offer some sort of percentage matching contribution. The most common that I have seen is a 3 percent match. This means that if you invest 3 percent of your income into the retirement plan, your employer will match that contribution with an additional 3 percent. Consider this match a raise. It is a reward for saving for your future.

I have worked with many small business owners over the years, and based on my experience, all want to see their employees succeed. They want to know that when their long-term employees leave the company, those employees will get to enjoy a comfortable retirement. Unfortunately, I have also discovered that while this matching contribution is an incredible incentive for any employee, many employees chose to not save into their company's work retirement plan. They want the money and are willing to forego the employer match and tax benefits. They choose not to take the raise or save for their futures. They want their cake now!

It is important to understand that investments in the tax-deferred bucket give you the most immediate recognized savings. Similar to choosing an apple in the fridge over the cake, you get an immediate benefit. With the apple, your body absorbs the natural sugars and gets a burst of energy. With the tax-deferred savings, you immediately see your total federal and state taxes go down. You also potentially enjoy a company match. So why would anyone decide not to contribute to a pre-tax retirement plan?

The simple answer is that these plans do come with some strings attached. One of the most critical limitations of pre-tax retirement plans involves your age. In most cases, money that goes into these plans should not be touched prior to age 59 and a half. If it is withdrawn prior to age 59 and a half, it is taxed at the employee's highest tax bracket with an additional 10 percent early withdrawal penalty assessed. This means that if someone is in the 22 percent federal bracket and also pays state taxes of 5 percent, they could see 37 percent of their plan distributions go toward taxes after the 10 percent penalty is assessed.

Try not to become too intimidated by the age restriction. Keep in mind that the purpose of this bucket is to encourage you to save money for your retirement and long-term goals. Imagine that you are retired after age 59 and a half, and you no longer have to save for retirement and your children's education goals. Imagine also that your mortgage and other liabilities are paid off. Your retirement income need is much lower, and because of this reduced income, your taxable income now falls into the 12 percent federal tax bracket. In this scenario, your pre-tax retirement plan distributions will be taxed at the 12 percent federal rate instead of the 22 percent pre-retirement rate. That's 10 percent of your income that you will never pay to the government. That's all money in your pocket! The question is, Can you survive without eating all the cake?

## TAX-FREE BUCKET

While the tax-deferred bucket does offer several immediate benefits, it is also important to remember the final bucket, otherwise referred to as the tax-free bucket. Similar to the taxable bucket, money that goes into this bucket has already been taxed, but the growth that takes place inside of the bucket is tax-free! Consider it the tuna fish in the fridge. It may not be quite as appetizing as the cake or the apple, but the benefit of the tuna fish is that its protein and nutrients will provide you with staying power and will help your muscles grow.

In the tax-free bucket the dividends, capital gains, and interest payments that you receive are never taxed if used properly. It almost sounds too good to be true, but like the tax-deferred bucket, the tax-free option has its restrictions, which can vary depending on the type of savings vehicle that you select.

## Roth IRA

The most popular tax-free savings vehicle is the Roth IRA. With the Roth IRA, money that you put into the account is after-tax money that you would pull from your checking or savings account. Like the traditional IRA, the maximum a person can put into a Roth IRA is $5,500 per year, or $6,500 if the individual is over age 50. So why is the Roth IRA so popular?

The answer has to do with the contributions or principal that you invest into the Roth. A unique feature of the Roth is that when you withdraw money from the account, you pull your principal out first before you pull any earnings. This means that if you invested $5,500 into a Roth IRA and it grew to $7,000, you could withdraw up to $5,500 from the Roth IRA at any time without any taxes owed or penalties.

### ROTH IRA CONTRIBUTIONS AND GAINS

Interest/Dividends/Gains:

$1,500

(Available Under Certain Conditions)

After-Tax Contributions/Principal:

$5,500

(Available Whenever Needed)

Once the principal is completely withdrawn, any additional pulls prior to age 59 and a half will be taxed as ordinary income with a 10 percent penalty. There are several exceptions and scenarios that allow a Roth IRA account holder to withdraw gains from the Roth IRA prior to age 59 and a half without paying the 10 percent penalty. (Taxes on the gains will still need to be paid.) These exceptions include:[1]

- For a first-time home purchase (with a $10,000 lifetime limit)
- If you become disabled
- As a result of your death, where the distributions are paid to a beneficiary
- For higher education expenses for yourself and/or eligible family members
- For unreimbursed medical expenses that exceed a certain percentage of your adjusted gross income
- For health insurance premiums if you are unemployed
- If the distributions are made in substantially equal periodic payments over the period of your life expectancy
- Due to an IRS levy
- For a qualified reservist distribution

The ability to withdraw the principal (and gains, under certain circumstances) from a Roth IRA adds incredible flexibility to your long-term savings strategy. I often encourage clients to view their Roth IRAs as a last resort emergency reserve, to be accessed only if all primary and secondary cash reserves are depleted.

Another advantage of the Roth IRA is that it does not require both spouses to work. As long as one spouse generates income, each spouse can set up and fund a Roth IRA.

It is important to note that there are modified adjusted gross income limits that can prevent you from funding a Roth IRA. In 2018 the modified AGI phase-out started at $120,000 for single

---

1 Internal Revenue Service. "Additional Tax on Early Distributions from Traditional and Roth IRAs." Tax Topic No. 557. www.irs.gov/taxtopics/tc557.html. Accessed November 1, 2017.

filers and went up to $135,000. For married filers, the phase-out ranged from $189,000 to $199,000. If your income exceeded these thresholds, you could not directly fund a Roth IRA. There are back-door methods to fund a Roth IRA, but those methods go beyond the teachings of this book. Tax advisors and financial planners can help you better understand these methods and determine whether they are available to you.

In addition to the Roth IRA, there are other tax-free growth vehicles that exist, each with its own unique features and restrictions. See the following bullet points for key features of some of these vehicles.

### Roth 401(k) / 403(b) Retirement Plans

- The savings in a Roth account should be viewed as retirement savings only.
- In 2018 the maximum annual contribution was $18,500, or $24,500 if you were over age 50. You can contribute to the Roth 401(k), the Traditional 401(k), or a combination of both up to the maximum level.
- Unlike the Roth IRA, you cannot gain access to the principal inside of the Roth 401(k) plan if distributions are made prior to age 59 and a half.

### 529 College Education Savings Plans

- The savings inside of the 529 plan should be viewed as strictly K-12 or college education savings. Money in these plans should not be used for retirement or other long-term goals.
- Most states offer their own 529 plans. Some states also offer a state tax incentive to their residents to fund the

state plan. Make sure to research whether your state offers a state tax deferral benefit before establishing one of these plans.

- When distributions are made from the 529 plan, the gains are pulled first and then the principal. This is the opposite of how distributions are viewed from a Roth IRA.
- In 529 plans, one adult is the owner and one child is the beneficiary. Although only one child's name is listed, funds inside of a traditional 529 plan can be used for the education expenses of anyone in the family, including siblings, spouse, and self. Funds inside of a custodial 529 plan must be used for the child named on the plan.
- The maximum annual contribution in 2018 was $15,000 per parent per beneficiary. This means that each parent could invest $15,000 annually into a 529 plan set up for one child.
- There is also a five-year rule with 529 plans that allows the 529 owner to contribute five years' worth of 529 plan contributions, or $75,000, all in one year without gifting penalties. If this strategy is used, the person making the contribution cannot make any additional contributions toward the beneficiary's 529 plan for the next five years.
- There are no maximum income limits to fund a 529 plan.

There are other "tax-free growth" investment vehicles, including Coverdell education savings accounts (ESAs), cash value life insurance policies, municipal bonds, Unified Trust to Minors Accounts (UTMAs), and residential real estate. They each have distinct characteristics, and it is highly advised that you speak with a financial planner or tax advisor before adding any of these vehicles to your long-term investment portfolio.

If you don't know what you are doing when you set up any of these tax-efficient investment accounts, the long-term impact could be the exact opposite of what you hoped to achieve. You wouldn't go to a gym and just start jumping on machines without fully understanding how each machine works. Likewise, with tax-planning strategies, make sure that you do your homework first and seek out specific advice before making any investments. If you decide that you want to try it on your own, you could start by prioritizing your use of tax-deferred and tax-free savings vehicles in the following manner:

1. Fund your pre-tax work retirement plan(s) up to the employer matching level.

2. Fully fund Roth IRAs up to the maximum levels for each spouse (assuming that your taxable income is below the income limit).

3. Increase your 401(k) savings up to the maximum level (assuming your taxable income falls in the 22 percent federal tax bracket or higher),

4. Determine whether there are additional tax-deferred savings vehicles, like a 457(b) retirement plan, available through your employer. If yes, contribute up to the plan's maximum, assuming that your taxable income still remains above the 22 percent federal tax bracket.

5. Consult a financial professional before you start directing your savings toward retirement and education savings vehicles outside of your work retirement plans and Roth IRAs.

## CHAPTER 6

# HIGH-INTEREST DEBT: THE STEROIDS OF FINANCIAL PLANNING

*"The pump [getting pumped up] is one of the better highs in life. You don't need to shoot up for it, you don't need to snort it. All you've got to do is sweat for it."*

**—GREG PLITT**

While creating a game plan to maximize tax efficiency can drastically improve your overall financial picture, there is one obstacle that cannot be overlooked. It is *debt*, specifically high-interest consumer debt, and it deserves a chapter all to itself. Just as I compared the Tax Control Triangle buckets to three food types (a slice of cake, an apple, and a plate of tuna fish), high-interest debt has its own corollary: it is the illicit drug of financial planning. It will eat away at the growth that your investments generate. It will strangle your cash flow. It will lead to fights, and if not addressed immediately, it will balloon into an uncontrollable monster that may sabotage your entire financial future!

An apt fitness analogy would be steroids. One of the most memorable videos on Greg's website is titled "Steroid Use at a Young Age." The video starts with a mother writing an email to Greg, telling him about her 15-year-old son who plays sports. She explains that a number of her son's teammates are trying steroids to build up their muscles and her son is starting to show interest. She is worried.

My confident cousin, who almost never showed signs of weakness or fear, had to hold back his emotions as he started to reflect on the situation. Greg knew just what the young man was experiencing. He also had to choose at that crossroad in his own life. Greg paused for a moment and stared into the camera as if he was speaking directly to her son.

Greg explained that the path of steroids is not the path of character. He stated, "You might have that trophy, but I'll tell you what: At those dark hours of the night after you have fooled everybody else into thinking that you are a great hero of the athletic field, in the middle of the night when you get up and go to the bathroom and look at yourself in the mirror and that image is looking back at you, will you be smiling then? Because you ended up fooling everyone else, and you ended up fooling yourself too, didn't you?"

Greg went on to explain, "That trophy stands there not because of your hard work and dedication or sacrifice. It stands there because you cut the corner. And later in life you are going to remember that lesson right there that you were rewarded with. You did the wrong thing and you got rewarded. You are going to think that you can do it again and again and again . . . I don't know when along the line it is going to catch up to you, but you are going to have to pay the price for your actions. I guarantee you that if it doesn't happen now, it is going to happen later in life where it's more than you paying that price."

Taking drugs can give people a sensation of satisfaction and happiness. Drugs can make people feel empowered. But the sensation is brief, and the consequences are almost always dire. Drugs can lead to brain damage, tumors, or even death. They can also lead to addiction. Once you get hooked on the short-term high, the temptation to keep making bad choices only grows.

The same logic is true when it comes to debt. Financial debt can fool people into believing that they have achieved some sense of financial security and stability. They experience the short-term high of making a purchase now, even if the funds are not available to cover that purchase. It is only later in life that they discover that this false sense of stability can be completely shattered as the debt balloons and the creditors come calling.

To be fair, it is important to understand that there are many different types of debt. These types include mortgages, home equity lines of credit, auto loans, student loans, credit cards, and personal loans. Some debts can be very good and, in some cases, necessary. For example, most people usually cannot purchase a new home without having to take out some type of mortgage. Going to college may also require some financial assistance. Both of these priorities add value and stability to a family's financial future, but having debts outside of these two areas can and often will lead to problems.

Many families go through life knowing that there are financial commitments looming on the horizon, but they refuse to acknowledge them. Instead, they allow these commitments to creep up on them and wreak havoc on their lives.

One of the best examples in finance is the purchase of a new car. In a dual-income family, it is possible that both spouses require transportation to get to and from work. This may mean that they each own a car. Based on my experience, new car purchases take place about every 8 to 12 years. Yes, some individuals are able to keep their cars in such great shape that they last longer than 12 years, but it is always a gamble.

Let's go back to our example couple, Mike and Jessica. They both work. Mike purchased his car five years ago, and Jessica purchased her car 10 years ago. Jessica knows that her car is on its last legs and that she will need to purchase a new car soon. Mike hopes to have another five years of car life left before his vehicle needs to be replaced.

If Jessica has the cash, she can purchase a new $25,000 car outright with no interest or impact to her cash flow. However, if Jessica does not have any savings set aside for the new car, she may be forced to take out an auto loan. Initially, the loan might look very attractive. The dealership may offer financing over a five-year period with an interest rate of 5 percent. With no down payment, the monthly payment would be $471.78.

Jessica may be enticed by such a seemingly low payment. It is much easier to part with $471.78 monthly than it is to part with $25,000 all at once. What Jessica does not see is all of the interest she is going to pay on the loan. If she multiplies her monthly payment of $471.78 by 12 months and then multiplies the new number by five years, she will discover that her new car will actually end up costing her $28,306.80. She will end up paying an extra $3,306.80 for the same car.

Would Jessica purchase the new car if its upfront cost was $28,306.80? It is possible. She needs the car. But what will Jessica have to sacrifice to pay out that extra $3,306.80? Will she have to reduce her annual dining or travel budget? Perhaps she will decide instead to cut back on her future retirement or education savings. No matter what, something must be sacrificed to make up the lost income.

So let's assume that Jessica does decide to finance the new car. She is thrilled. She has a brand-new car with all the bells and whistles, and she didn't need to put any money down. That cash reserve that was set aside for the purchase of the car is now available for other potential purchases.

Mike and Jessica realize that this car will be perfect for camping excursions, so they drive over to the camping store, where they purchase a trailer and some gear. The total cost is $10,000. The camping gear costs were not in the original family budget. While Mike and Jessica could use the cash that was set aside for the car to cover the camping costs, they instead put the $10,000 on a credit card currently charging an 18 percent interest rate. They are excited to discover that the card has a low monthly payment of $150. They review their budget and determine that they can handle both the auto loan and the monthly credit card payments.

What Mike and Jessica don't realize is that they are falling into a debt trap. They are enjoying the emotional high of having their new car and all of their new camping equipment. They are starting to imagine all of the trips that they are going to take, but behind the scenes, the high-interest credit card debt is rapidly crippling their financial futures. They may not realize it at the time, but if they pay only $150 monthly toward their credit card balance, they will have that payment for the next 50-plus years! In total, they will end up paying over $80,000 in interest for the camping equipment that was originally sold for $10,000. Jessica may be able to justify the car, but there is no justification for paying $80,000 for camping equipment that originally cost $10,000.

As stated earlier, debt gives you a false sense of net worth. It allows you to think that you have something that in reality is not yours. If you don't pay your debts, you will soon discover that property can be repossessed, wages can be garnished, and respect can be lost. To make matters worse, debt will act as a virus that will eat away at the overall growth of your investments.

In addition to financial hardship, debt also may take a crippling emotional toll on your family. Couples in debt tend to fight, and their children are likely to listen and learn. If they see you fighting over money or blaming each other when it comes to debt, as adults they may respond to debt in a similar manner.

Lastly, uncontrolled debt will tarnish your credit score. Your credit score is the number that lenders use to help them decide how likely it is that they will be repaid on time if they give you a loan or a credit card. The FICO score is one of the most common types of credit scores. It can fall within a range of 300 to 850. Scores above 670 are considered good, and those above 800 are considered exceptional. A poor credit score often leads to higher-interest loans, or in more extreme cases, no loans at all. You become too great a risk for the lender. The factors that impact your credit score include:[1]

---

1 Experian Information Solutions. "What Is a Good Credit Score?" www.experian. com/blogs/ask-experian/credit-education/score-basics/what-is-a-good-credit-score/. Accessed November 1, 2017.

- Payment history for loans and credit cards
- Credit utilization rate
- Type, number, and age of credit accounts
- Total debt
- Public records such as bankruptcy, civil judgements, or tax liens
- Number of new credit accounts you have recently opened
- Number of inquiries for your credit report

There are three primary credit-reporting companies that monitor your credit:

| COMPANY | WEBSITE | PHONE |
| --- | --- | --- |
| Experian | www.experian.com | 1-888-397-3742 |
| Equifax | www.equifax.com | 1-866-349-5191 |
| TransUnion | www.transunion.com | 1-800-916-8800 |

It is prudent to annually request credit reports to confirm where your credit stands and determine whether there are any unexpected variations. You can call a single number to get the reports from all three companies, for free, once every 12 months: 1-877-322-8228. Each company provides a report that highlights the specific criteria that impact your credit score. This information will help you to pinpoint what areas need to be improved. You can also determine whether any corrections need to be made.

If you currently have high-interest credit card or other consumer debt, create a game plan with your spouse to get it paid off as quickly as possible. You may have to make some short-term sacrifices, but think of the freedom they will grant you in the long term. Paying down your debts improves your lives, your credit scores, and your futures, just like eating well and working out improves your health and well-being. You just need to make that choice on where your commitments and priorities truly stand.

**CHAPTER 7**

# YOUR HOME, YOUR GYM: WHAT DO YOU CONTROL?

*"Do you want to be a servant or a master of your own life?"*

**—GREG PLITT**

While debt can be deadly, it also can give you the opportunity to gain control over your life. We know that there are certain necessities in life that we all require in order to survive. Food, water, and shelter, for example, are absolutes. We are fortunate that in our society we have choices within each of these categories. For example, when you go to the grocery store, you have aisles of different food products and beverages at your disposal.

The same is true of shelter. When it comes to finding a place for your family to live, you have all sorts of options. You can rent an apartment, a condo, or a single-family home, or you can purchase a new home. Home ownership is one of the most significant and critical financial decisions that couples need to make in their lifetimes.

A unique way to view the benefits of home ownership is to use a fitness analogy. If you wish to develop a muscular physique, it is possible to achieve your goal without ever going to the gym. You can work out each day doing push-ups, sit-ups, squats, and other at-home cardio activities. You can run around the neighborhood or purchase some basic weights to keep in the house. You may be able to achieve your goal, but the time it will take to reach your target physique will likely be longer than you originally expected.

The advantage of going to a gym is that the gym provides access to all sorts of exercise equipment that will help you target particular muscle groups. You can do exercises that you can't do at home. You can lift weights that exceed your personal body weight. Depending on what features are available at the gym, you can try unique physical exercises such as swimming, rock climbing, and rowing. You can create a game plan that will allow you to target the exact muscle groups you want to improve, giving you the ability to reach your target physique goals in a much shorter period of time.

You can also choose which gym is best to meet your specific needs and goals. All sorts of gyms exist, each with its own unique features and amenities. If you plan to become a triathlete, you will need a gym that has a pool, stationary bikes, and treadmills. If your goal is muscle growth for body-sculpting competitions, you will want a gym with appropriate free weights and muscle-targeting machines. You do not need to join the largest gym in the neighborhood with a personal spa, restaurant, tanning beds, and foot rub stations. The gym, like everything in your life, should have a purpose.

This same logic applies to purchasing a home. Originally, home ownership was part of the American dream, but that dream diminished as couples started to forget the purpose of owning a home. Instead of focusing on the essential benefits of their new home—including shelter, safety, stability, community, and control—many buyers began focusing more heavily on the unessential amenities of the house. How big is the master bedroom? Does the backyard have a pool? Does the homeowners' association include a country club? How many spare rooms do we get? Are the counters granite and the floors tile? Where is the screened-in porch?

This focus on amenities led to people purchasing houses that they could not afford. Banks magnified this issue by offering mortgages with little to no money down. When people could not afford the fixed mortgage payment, the bank was quick to offer an alternative lower monthly payment with an adjustable rate mortgage, otherwise known as an ARM.

Then the great recession of 2008 struck, and families discovered that their wonderful new homes had morphed into debt traps with ballooning interest rates. Children watched as their parents struggled to keep up with mortgage payments or faced foreclosures and bankruptcies. The promise of shelter, safety, and stability withered. Now many young families take on the idea of home ownership with a great deal of skepticism and caution.

Many of my younger clients wonder whether home ownership is worth the risk. They ask a lot of questions: What if we need to move in five years? What if we have another recession next year and the home value goes down? What if we need to sell the house and can't? These are all valid questions, but the fear of "what if" scenarios should never prevent someone from making a decision. Families still need a place to live. Choosing not to purchase a home and instead to rent for the rest of your life is making a decision, and more than likely, it will be a costly one. Home ownership, if done properly, provides couples and families with an incredible amount of control in their financial lives.

For example, when a couple rents, they are at the mercy of their landlord. They have no control over their rent. Every time that their lease expires, they run the risk of rent increases or possibly being forced out of their home. They also have limited control over what they can do inside of their home. Remodeling the apartment to suit a family's changing needs may not be an option. They are restricted to the rules of their landlord, and the rent never stops! It will be a permanent part of their monthly cash flow for the rest of their lives.

Home ownership gives families the opportunity to choose, but more importantly, it provides them with greater control in their financial lives. With a fixed mortgage, couples know exactly what their monthly payment is going to be and when the payments will eventually stop. There are no payment increases, at least when it comes to the principal and interest. Granted, there are additional expenses in owning a home, but based on my experience, those additional expenses are often incorporated into the monthly rents charged on apartments, condos, and single-family homes.

Many couples are shocked when they see how much of a difference owning a home versus renting makes to their retirement analysis. It can cut years off of an estimated retirement date simply because the mortgage payment eventually ends. You will one day own your home. With rent, every payment is lost and no equity is ever built.

For example, if you purchase a home with a $200,000 30-year fixed mortgage at 4 percent interest, you will have a monthly principal and interest payment of $954.83. After 30 years, you will have paid out a total of $343,739.01. That number may seem significant, but consider the alternative. If you instead choose to rent with a monthly payment of $950, and the rent increases with inflation at a conservative rate of just 1 percent per year, after 30 years you will have paid out $396,547.80. To make matters worse, you will still need a place to live during your retirement years. After another 30 years, you will have paid out a total of $931,034.02 in rent:

**TOTAL PAYMENTS AFTER 60 YEARS**

You might argue that the additional costs of home upkeep and repair, real estate taxes, homeowner's insurance, and other home ownership expenses need to be factored into the calculation. While these expenses are important to consider, it is also important to recognize the following additional benefits of home ownership.

First, once the house is paid off, you now own your home. It is an asset with value, and hopefully has appreciated in value over the past 30 years. If needed, you can gain access to the equity in your home by setting up a home equity line of credit, establishing a reverse mortgage, or even selling the home.

Second, your mortgage interest can be tax deductible at both the state and federal levels if you itemize when filing your taxes. A $200,000 mortgage with a 4 percent interest rate incurs initially about $8,000 in interest per year. If you are in the 22 percent federal income tax bracket and the 5 percent state income tax bracket, claiming that interest as a deduction would reduce your federal taxes owed by $1,760 and state taxes owed by $400. The net effect is that you will have paid $5,840 after receiving the tax savings—reducing the mortgage's interest rate to about 2.92 percent. That looks a lot more attractive than the original 4 percent.

Third, you are in control. There is no landlord to price gouge you or kick you out of your home. You have the freedom and flexibility to maintain your home as you see fit.

Fourth, we are in a unique time in US history. Mortgage rates have a direct correlation with the US government's 10-year treasury rate. It is often referred to as the "prime" interest rate. As shown in the following chart,[1] the 10-year yield has been dropping sharply since the 1980s. It hit its peak back in September 1981 at 15.32 percent.

1 Multpl.com. "Ten-Year Treasury Rate." www.multpl.com/10-year-treasury-rate/table/by-year. Accessed January 14, 2018.

## TEN-YEAR TREASURY RATE ON JANUARY 1 BY DECADE

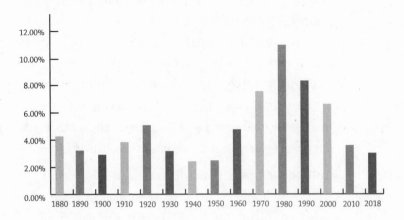

Back then, many new homeowners faced mortgage rates as high 14 percent. Fast forward to July 2016, and the yield plummeted to its lowest level in US history, at 1.5 percent. As of January 1, 2018, the rate went back up only slightly, to 2.5 percent. Recent new homeowners who have refinanced their existing mortgages or made new purchases have been able to acquire new 30-year fixed mortgage rates for 3.5 percent or, in some extreme cases, even lower.

It is very possible that mortgage rates may never be this low again in our lifetimes! Locking in a long-term mortgage with such low rates now could prove to be a very cost-efficient strategy over the long term. When you are ready to consider your options for purchasing a new home or possibly refinancing an existing loan, here are a few key points to consider:

- Home ownership is about control. One of the easiest ways to give up that control is to purchase an adjustable rate mortgage, or ARM. With an ARM, your rate is locked for a period, but at the end of that period, the rate can start to balloon quickly, sending your monthly mortgage payment skyrocketing. As shown in the Ten-Year Treasury Rate chart, we are hovering near the lowest interest rates in US history. Do you think that rates are likely to go up or down in the future? Chances are high that rates will go up, leaving you in a very difficult position when the ARM period ends. Stick with a fixed mortgage and a consistent monthly payment.

- Another acronym that affects your level of control is PMI, which stands for private mortgage insurance. This is an insurance premium that you pay on top of your monthly mortgage payment if you are not able to apply a large enough down payment on the home. It is insurance meant to protect the bank, not you, if you are unable to keep up with your monthly mortgage payments. Usually the required down payment to avoid PMI is 20 percent of the value of the home.

My rule of thumb is to estimate the cost of a new home in your desired area and what the required 20 percent down payment would be. Once you know that number, save every available penny toward the target down payment before you begin searching for a new home. My three exceptions to this rule are if you have not yet achieved your cash reserve target goal, if you are not yet taking advantage of an employer-matched work retirement plan, and if you have debt with an interest rate exceeding 4 percent. Your surplus cash flow should be directed toward those categories, in the order listed above, before the home purchase down payment.

- If you can't wait to build the 20 percent down payment and need to purchase a new home sooner with PMI, make sure that once the new home is purchased, you dedicate surplus cash flow toward the mortgage until the PMI is removed (following the same rule and exceptions listed above).

- Clients often ask me if they should put more toward their mortgage than the required minimum monthly payment. This can be done by either increasing their monthly mortgage payment or paying the mortgage biweekly instead of monthly. While some television or radio personalities recommend trying to pay off all your debt as quickly as possible, I disagree. Study after study shows that it is a far more effective strategy to apply the minimum required payment toward your mortgage and direct the excess available cash flow toward your long-term investments.

  Over a 15- or 30-year period, a properly allocated long-term investment portfolio should be able to achieve a much higher rate of return than what is being paid out on the mortgage. Also, putting too much money into your home reduces your financial flexibility. If all your money is tied up in the house and you need funds to help with large, lump-sum expenses like college education, trying to pull it from your home equity may be costly and restrictive. Keep your options open and invest your excess cash flow using the tax-efficient savings strategies outlined in chapter 5.

**CHAPTER 8**

# YOUR LONG-TERM GOALS: PRIORITIES OR EXCUSES?

*"You are what you do repeatedly. If excellence is something you're striving for, then it's not an accident. It's a habit."*

**—GREG PLITT**

Everything that you have read up to this point has focused on the essentials of financial planning. You have read about identifying and prioritizing your financial goals; creating detailed net worth and cash flow statements; developing an efficient cash reserve; addressing your life, income, and estate protection needs; identifying tax-efficient savings strategies; and determining how best to approach your home purchase goal. The previous chapters give you a strong foundation from which you can work confidently toward your long-term financial goals.

Everything you are about to read will have little to no value if you do not follow the guidance provided in the previous chapters. As stated at the beginning of this book, trying to plan for your long-term goals without first addressing the foundation of your financial situation is a recipe for both confusion and failure. Don't make the mistake of skipping steps. Follow the suggested guidelines, and you will find the overall planning process much easier to handle.

Once you are ready to begin planning for your future goals, make sure to identify and agree with your partner on which goals have the highest priority. For most families, the two most critical long-term financial goals are retirement planning and education planning. If we go back to the cash flow breakdown example with Mike and Jessica, we see those goals listed on the right-hand side in Stage Two:

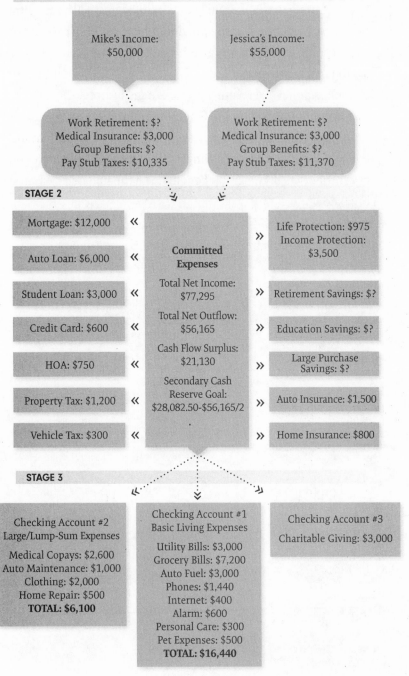

**STAGE 1**

Mike's Income:
$50,000

Jessica's Income:
$55,000

Work Retirement: $?
Medical Insurance: $3,000
Group Benefits: $?
Pay Stub Taxes: $10,335

Work Retirement: $?
Medical Insurance: $3,000
Group Benefits: $?
Pay Stub Taxes: $11,370

**STAGE 2**

Mortgage: $12,000 «

Auto Loan: $6,000 «

Student Loan: $3,000 «

Credit Card: $600 «

HOA: $750 «

Property Tax: $1,200 «

Vehicle Tax: $300 «

**Committed Expenses**

Total Net Income:
$77,295

Total Net Outflow:
$56,165

Cash Flow Surplus:
$21,130

Secondary Cash
Reserve Goal:
$28,082.50-$56,165/2

» Life Protection: $975
Income Protection:
$3,500

» Retirement Savings: $?

» Education Savings: $?

» Large Purchase
Savings: $?

» Auto Insurance: $1,500

» Home Insurance: $800

**STAGE 3**

Checking Account #2
Large/Lump-Sum Expenses

Medical Copays: $2,600
Auto Maintenance: $1,000
Clothing: $2,000
Home Repair: $500
**TOTAL: $6,100**

Checking Account #1
Basic Living Expenses

Utility Bills: $3,000
Grocery Bills: $7,200
Auto Fuel: $3,000
Phones: $1,440
Internet: $400
Alarm: $600
Personal Care: $300
Pet Expenses: $500
**TOTAL: $16,440**

Checking Account #3

Charitable Giving: $3,000

Assuming that Mike and Jessica have addressed the essential planning areas listed in the previous chapters, they can update their cash flow breakdown to include their work retirement savings up to the matching levels and their individual life and disability policy premiums. Two changes of note: their Group Benefits line item in Stage One now reflects $0 going toward group benefits, and their pay stub taxes have gone down due to their increased pretax savings. Mike and Jessica's employers cover the costs of the group benefits. See the updated cash flow breakdown:

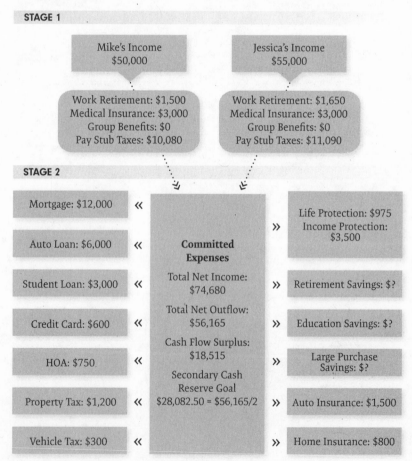

**STAGE 1**

Mike's Income
$50,000

Jessica's Income
$55,000

Work Retirement: $1,500
Medical Insurance: $3,000
Group Benefits: $0
Pay Stub Taxes: $10,080

Work Retirement: $1,650
Medical Insurance: $3,000
Group Benefits: $0
Pay Stub Taxes: $11,090

**STAGE 2**

Mortgage: $12,000 «

Auto Loan: $6,000 «

Student Loan: $3,000 «

Credit Card: $600 «

HOA: $750 «

Property Tax: $1,200 «

Vehicle Tax: $300 «

**Committed Expenses**

Total Net Income:
$74,680

Total Net Outflow:
$56,165

Cash Flow Surplus:
$18,515

Secondary Cash
Reserve Goal
$28,082.50 = $56,165/2

» Life Protection: $975
Income Protection: $3,500

» Retirement Savings: $?

» Education Savings: $?

» Large Purchase Savings: $?

» Auto Insurance: $1,500

» Home Insurance: $800

You will notice that the cash flow surplus is now reduced to $18,515. This remaining cash flow is the money that Mike and Jessica can choose to dedicate toward their long-term goals or toward their Stage Three committed and discretionary spending buckets. Now comes the time when they must make a choice: Do they value their long-term goals more or less than their current spending luxuries? The same question awaits you.

You are almost always in control of the choice. You can wake up each morning and go to the gym or hit the snooze button and sleep for another hour. You can open the fridge and choose the bottled water or the chocolate milk. This same mentality applies in finance. You get to choose whether you will place your future goals above your present desires. The results will be the same, though the timing is different: gratification now or gratification later.

Usually, when it comes to addressing long-term goals, the priorities should be listed in order of timeline, starting with the shortest-term goals, like a home purchase, and ending with retirement. It is important to note that the education goal does not apply to this thought process. You may have heard the saying that you can borrow for your education goals, but you cannot borrow for retirement.

I have discovered that financial stability, especially in retirement years, is a gift not to just the retirees, but to their grown children as well. Put more bluntly, the long-term financial stability of a parent gives an adult child peace of mind, knowing that he or she will likely not be required to provide additional monetary support to that parent in later years. To give your children that freedom, make sure to fully address your retirement planning needs before working toward your education savings goals.

## RETIREMENT

To determine exactly how much you will need to retire comfortably is a challenging task, especially during your younger years. So many variables can impact your retirement projections, including inflation, changes to tax law, unforeseen future lump-sum expenses, and unknown life expectancies. While there are online calculators to give you a sense of what your target retirement asset number might look like, I often find that these calculators are misleading. They can give a false sense of financial security or make things seem so unobtainable that some families just give up hope.

The reason that these calculators are misleading is that they make too many general assumptions. They may ask for statistics including current age, current income, current living expenses, current savings level, estimated rate of return, and target retirement age. While this information is helpful, it only skims the surface of all of the factors that go into determining a family's retirement asset need. Other variables that are often overlooked include liabilities, Social Security income, possible pension income, how retirement assets are currently invested from a taxation standpoint, and outside income sources like rental properties.

To give a clearer example of how these variables play a significant role in determining a family's preparedness for retirement, let's assume that two different couples use the same online calculator. Their ages are the same. Neither family has children. The household income for both families is the same. The total liabilities are the same. On the surface everything looks equal. But after taking a closer look at each family's net worth and cash flow statements, some major discrepancies start to appear:

- Family A is a dual-income family with both spouses making about equal pay. In Family B only the wife works. This variation in income sources will have a significant impact on how Social Security benefits are paid out in retirement.

- Family A has a mortgage that will be paid off in 10 years. Family B does not own a home; it rents. Given this information, Family A will have its home paid off before retirement, while Family B may continue to have rental payments throughout the retirement years. The continued rental payments will rapidly eat away at the couple's retirement assets.

There are numerous other examples of how analyzing a family's financial standing and retirement goals using only basic information can lead to incomplete or even inaccurate guidance. In order to gain a clearer understanding of what your family needs to do to retire comfortably, consider working with a financial planner who can provide a comprehensive view of your unique situation. The key word is *comprehensive*. A financial planner can use software that takes into account all of the information on your net worth and cash flow statements as well as other information outside of the statements, like Social Security, real estate income, and pension income. The advisor can also adjust variables in your personal analysis, including inflation rates, life expectancies, retirement dates, discretionary cash flow changes, estimated rates of return, and more. Determining how to locate and interview a financial planner is discussed in chapter 10, but for now, we will stick with a more simplistic retirement savings strategy.

Before any surplus cash flow is dedicated toward long-term savings, all excess available cash flow should first be directed toward building a solid secondary cash reserve and paying off any consumer debts with interest rates above 4 percent. Refer back to Mike and Jessica's net worth statement from chapter 2:

## MIKE AND JESSICA'S NET WORTH STATEMENT

| ASSETS | | | |
|---|---|---|---|
| TYPE | AMOUNT | EST. RATE OF RETURN | PURPOSE |
| Checking Account | $1,000 | .06% | Cash Reserve |
| Savings Account | $4,000 | .1% | Cash Reserve |
| Work 401(k) Plan (M) | $10,000 | 7%–10% | Retirement |
| Retirement Plan (J) | $5,000 | 7%–10% | Retirement |
| IRA (J) | $10,000 | 7%–10% | Retirement |
| 529 Plan | $2,000 | 7%–10% | Education |
| Joint Investment Account | $24,000 | 7%–10% | Education |
| House | $250,000 | n/a | Personal |
| Car | $20,000 | n/a | Personal |
| TOTAL ASSETS | $326,000 | | |

| LIABILITIES | | |
|---|---|---|
| TYPE | AMOUNT | INTEREST CHARGED |
| Mortgage | $200,000 | 4% |
| Auto Loan | $10,000 | 4.9% |
| Student Loan | $8,000 | 8% |
| Credit Card Balance | $3,000 | 18% |
| TOTAL LIABILITIES | $221,000 | |
| NET WORTH | $105,000 ($326,000 – $221,000) | |

Mike and Jessica will want to pay off their auto loan, student loan, and credit card balance as quickly as possible:

> Auto Loan: $6,000

> Student Loan: $3,000

> Credit Card: $600

To address their secondary cash reserve need of $28,082.50, they might consider redeeming or selling the investments in their joint taxable investment account and directing the cash toward their secondary reserves in the Committed Expenses account.

Then, based on their annual cash flow surplus of $18,515, they should be able to pay off the liabilities in less than a year and a half. After the liabilities are paid off, they can eliminate from their cash flow breakdown the monthly payments dedicated toward those liabilities and redirect the newly available cash toward their annual cash flow surplus total.

After the consumer debts are paid off and reserve needs are met, I often propose that families save a minimum of 15 percent of their gross income toward long-term retirement goals. Research from multiple sources (including the Center for Retirement Research at Boston College[1]) has shown that this savings level is appropriate for middle-income families. Let's use Mike and Jessica to illustrate this retirement savings target. They are already saving $3,150 annually in their work retirement plans, and they are also receiving a 100 percent match on their contributions, which doubles the annual savings to $6,300.

---

1 Alicia H. Munnell, Anthony Webb, and Wenliang Hou. "How Much Should People Save?" Issue in Brief No. 14-11 (July 2014), Center for Retirement Research at Boston College. http://crr.bc.edu/wp-content/uploads/2014/07/IB_14-111.pdf. Accessed January 14, 2018.

Without any additional savings, they are already dedicating 6 percent of their income toward retirement savings! To reach 15 percent, they will need to save an additional $9,450.

If Mike and Jessica want to make use of the Tax Control Triangle (see chapter 5), they will need to first determine their taxable income. They make a gross income of $105,000. Their medical premiums of $6,000 are tax deductible, and they can take advantage of the standard married tax deduction of $24,000. Once they subtract the medical premiums and standard deduction from their gross income, their taxable income lands at $75,000. The married filing jointly 12 percent federal tax bracket caps at $77,400. See again the 2018 federal tax brackets:

| TAX RATE | INCOME RANGE |
|----------|--------------|
| 10% | $0 to $19,050 |
| 12% | $19,051 to $77,400 |
| 22% | $77,401 to $165,000 |
| 24% | $165,001 to $315,00 |
| 32% | $315,001 to $400,000 |
| 35% | $400,001 to $600,000 |
| 37% | $600,001 + |

Mike and Jessica have no current income that falls in the 22 percent federal bracket. Recognizing that it is very unlikely that they will pay less than 12 percent in federal tax in retirement, they decide to fully fund Roth IRAs at $5,500 each to take advantage of the Roth IRA's tax-free growth. The Roth IRA savings combined with their 401(k) savings and match brings their overall retirement savings percentage to about 16.5 percent! See the updated Stage Two cash flow breakdown reflecting the added retirement savings:

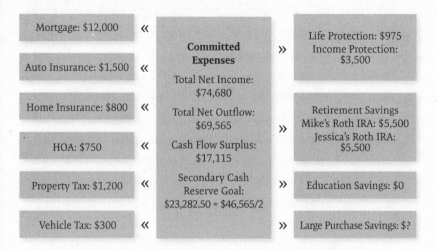

| Mortgage: $12,000 | « | **Committed Expenses** | » | Life Protection: $975 Income Protection: $3,500 |
| Auto Insurance: $1,500 | « | Total Net Income: $74,680 | | |
| Home Insurance: $800 | « | Total Net Outflow: $69,565 | » | Retirement Savings Mike's Roth IRA: $5,500 Jessica's Roth IRA: $5,500 |
| HOA: $750 | « | Cash Flow Surplus: $17,115 | | |
| Property Tax: $1,200 | « | Secondary Cash Reserve Goal: $23,282.50 = $46,565/2 | » | Education Savings: $0 |
| Vehicle Tax: $300 | « | | » | Large Purchase Savings: $? |

You may have also noticed that in Stage Two, the auto loan, student loan, and credit card liabilities have been paid off and thus removed. Mike and Jessica have eliminated $9,600 in liabilities while adding $11,000 in retirement savings, increasing their net outflow only slightly. They still have $17,115 in annual surplus cash flow available. This surplus cash flow can be directed toward one or a combination of the following three areas:

- Their overall retirement savings
- Their other long-term savings goals, including education and the purchase of a bigger home
- Their Stage Three checking accounts to increase their current standard of living

They still have the choice. What would you do?

## OTHER MID- TO LONG-TERM GOALS

When originally listing their goals, Mike and Jessica stated that they also wanted to address the following priorities: the purchase of a new car, education planning for a future family, and the purchase of a bigger home. The new car and new home goals are shorter-term goals that they plan to tackle in the next few years. While these goals were listed as higher priorities than retirement, you may notice that my suggestions up to this point have prioritized high-interest debt elimination, building a strong cash reserve, addressing protection needs, and retirement planning above both of these goals as well as their long-term education goal.

The reason for this shift in prioritization has everything to do with flexibility. As stated earlier, my most successful clients are the ones who systematize as much as possible and incorporate flexibility as often as possible into their overall planning. So how does flexibility apply here?

### Car Purchase

Let's start with the new car purchase goal. Mike and Jessica stated that they will likely need to purchase a new $25,000 car in the next year.

They have multiple options to pay for the car. They can use their cash reserves and then focus on rebuilding the reserves once the car is purchased. They can take out an auto loan if the financing options are attractive, or they may be able to set up a home equity line of credit (HELOC) and use it to cover the car expense. If none of these options sounds attractive, they can turn to their Roth IRAs. As discussed in chapter 5, the principal in Roth IRAs can be withdrawn at any time for any reason, but once it is pulled, it cannot be replenished. Therefore, it is prudent to consider withdrawals from your Roth IRAs a last resort before turning toward high-interest consumer debt.

### Home Purchase

The reason that the home purchase goal was not placed above retirement is that they already own a home. Let's revisit the chapter 7 discussion about purchasing a new home. Before Mike and Jessica consider moving into a new home, especially if it is a larger, more expensive home, they need to first confirm the rationale for moving. Is it for necessity, or is it for convenience?

Many people skip all of the steps we have discussed up to this point. They neglect the debt elimination and the building of their cash reserves. They procrastinate in addressing their life and income protection needs. They ignore their long-term retirement planning goals. Ignoring all of these priorities can leave a family with a very healthy-looking cash flow. Clients are often surprised at just how much banks are willing to lend to them for a new home purchase. It is important to understand that lenders do not care if you are on track for retirement. They are not worried if you have not addressed your protection needs. They may be concerned about your cash reserves, but only because they want some assurance that the monthly mortgage bill will continue to be paid. They are not concerned about your long-term goals, and they are not supposed to be. Your family's goals and priorities are the responsibility of you and your spouse.

So before purchasing a larger home, make sure that your other planning goals are on track and that your new home will not force you to make sacrifices that could harm you and your family now or in the future!

## Education Planning

Education planning is one of the most emotional financial decisions a family needs to make. Couples can have very different opinions on what is appropriate in terms of helping their children with college education expenses. Oftentimes, these differences in opinion are the result of different upbringings. One spouse may have attended four years of college paid for by his parents while the other may have not attended college or had to cover tuition costs on her own. Some parents feel that it is important for children to experience the financial burden of college expenses to help them appreciate both the education and the value of money. Other parents don't want their children to worry about anything but their studies.

There is no right or wrong answer to how to approach education planning, but it, like all other long-term goals, needs to be discussed, and a goal needs to be set. Our example couple, Mike and Jessica, do not have children. Their goal is to start a family and hopefully have two children in the next five years. While children are not yet part of their family structure, discussing their goals for family planning and education now will help them avoid complications later.

Education goals do not have the same timeline flexibility as retirement. Usually, children go to college as soon as they finish high school. This means that once a child is born, parents have approximately 18 years before the first tuition bills come due. The difficulty is determining how much those tuition bills and other college expenses will be. Today, overall college expenses can range from a few thousand dollars a year to more than $76,000 a year when you include additional expenses like room and board. The uncertainty of the future costs makes education planning very intimidating. The high inflationary rise in college costs also adds to the problem.

Rather than turn a blind eye, parents should sit down and discuss what minimum level of support they wish to provide for their children's education needs. They may not be able to afford a $76,000 annual tuition, but funding a $25,000 in-state tuition may be more feasible.

Using the example of Mike and Jessica, if they assume that they will have a child in the next year and another in three years, they can then estimate that they will need to start covering college expenses in 18 years. They determine that they would like to cover four years of college education for each child at $25,000 annually in today's dollars. They also assume that college costs will rise at a 6 percent rate of inflation. After consulting with a financial planner, they project that they will need to accumulate a total of $312,166 over 18 years for their first child and $350,750 over 20 years for their second child.

It is important that you make sure not to focus on the big future numbers! Instead, focus on the monthly amount that you will need to save to achieve the college education goals. Greg used to often say, "The real reason that people quit is because they focus on the distance they have to travel." Mike and Jessica have time on their hands. They also have the freedom to change their education goals in the future if ever needed or desired.

Again, with the help of a financial planner, Mike and Jessica determine that if they save monthly for their education goals and invest the savings into funds that yield an average 8 percent rate of return, they would need to save $650.23 monthly to cover the first child's college education need and $595.48 monthly to cover the second child's college education need. This total savings would amount to $14,948.52 annually between now and college.

That annual savings may seem significant, but when we revisit their cash flow breakdown spreadsheet, we can see that they have $17,115 available to dedicate toward their future goals:

**Committed Expenses**

Total Net Income:
$74,680

Total Net Outflow:
$69,565

Cash Flow Surplus:
$17,115

Secondary Cash Reserve Goal
(Does Not Include Savings):
$23,282.50 = $46,565/2

Mike and Jessica do not yet have children, so they will want to make sure that they don't dedicate their cash flow surplus to investment vehicles (like 529 plans and Coverdell ESAs) that are restricted to only education expenses. These savings should remain flexible and accessible when needed. In the future, if they do not end up having children, they may decide to redirect that money to the other savings goals like a new car, a new home, or possibly their retirement.

Mike and Jessica decide to set up a regular "non-qualified" (taxable) investment account and invest $916.67 monthly into the account, for an annual total of $11,000. While this systematic savings covers only about 74 percent of their education savings goal, they recognize that they could also tap into their Roth IRAs to help cover college education expenses if needed or desired. They also understand that the savings in the non-qualified account and the Roth IRAs can be used to help cover short-term expenses or lump sum needs if necessary. See the updated cash flow breakdown in Stages Two and Three:

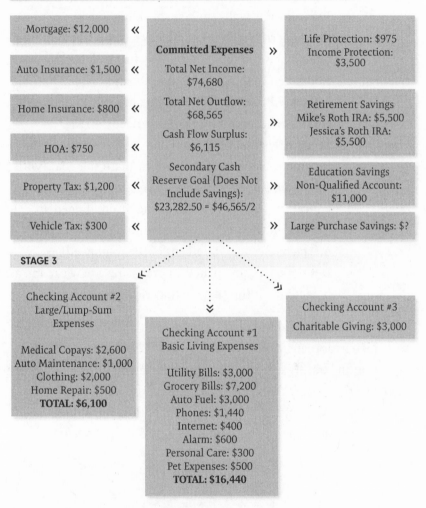

**STAGE 2**

Mortgage: $12,000 «

Auto Insurance: $1,500 «

Home Insurance: $800 «

HOA: $750 «

Property Tax: $1,200 «

Vehicle Tax: $300 «

**Committed Expenses** »

Total Net Income: $74,680

Total Net Outflow: $68,565 »

Cash Flow Surplus: $6,115

Secondary Cash Reserve Goal (Does Not Include Savings): » $23,282.50 = $46,565/2

»

Life Protection: $975
Income Protection: $3,500

Retirement Savings
Mike's Roth IRA: $5,500
Jessica's Roth IRA: $5,500

Education Savings
Non-Qualified Account: $11,000

Large Purchase Savings: $?

**STAGE 3**

Checking Account #2
Large/Lump-Sum Expenses

Medical Copays: $2,600
Auto Maintenance: $1,000
Clothing: $2,000
Home Repair: $500
**TOTAL: $6,100**

Checking Account #1
Basic Living Expenses

Utility Bills: $3,000
Grocery Bills: $7,200
Auto Fuel: $3,000
Phones: $1,440
Internet: $400
Alarm: $600
Personal Care: $300
Pet Expenses: $500
**TOTAL: $16,440**

Checking Account #3
Charitable Giving: $3,000

Notice that they still have $6,115 in surplus annual cash flow. Following the steps listed in the previous chapters, at this point, they have accomplished the following:

- Paid off their high-interest consumer debts
- Built up a cash reserve equal to six months' worth of their total Committed Expenses outflow (not including savings)
- Addressed their life protection needs
- Addressed their disability or income protection needs
- Addressed their estate planning needs
- Set up a systematic savings of over 15 percent of their income toward their retirement planning goal (with the flexibility of being able to rededicate funds from education savings vehicles in the future if needed)
- Addressed their education planning needs (currently on track to cover 74 percent of the total need)
- Developed a game plan for purchasing a new car and a new home, if they decide that either is necessary

All of their original goals have been addressed except for taking vacations. Their goal was to spend $2,000 annually on vacation and travel expenses. Using their remaining surplus cash flow of $6,115, they then decide to increase their annual allotment from the Committed Expenses account to their Stage Three Large/Lump-Sum Expenses account by $2,000 for vacations/travel:

Checking Account #2
Large/Lump-Sum Expenses

Medical Copays: $2,600
Auto Maintenance: $1,000
Clothing: $2,000
Home Repair: $500
Vacation/Travel: $2,000
**TOTAL: $8,100**

After deducting the travel expenses from their surplus cash flow, they still have $4,115 available to dedicate toward discretionary spending. All of their future goals and needs have been addressed! They now can revisit their list of discretionary expenses to determine how they would like to allocate their remaining cash flow. Below are the discretionary expenses they had listed in their cash flow statement:

| DISCRETIONARY SPENDING | |
| --- | --- |
| Dining and Recreation | ? |
| Vacations | $2,000 |
| Gym Memberships | ? |
| Gifts to Family | ? |
| Video Streaming Service | ? |
| TOTAL DISCRETIONARY SPENDING | $6,115 |

Mike and Jessica take time together to determine which of these discretionary expenses are most important to them and their family. They allocate the surplus funds in the following manner:

| DISCRETIONARY SPENDING | |
| --- | --- |
| Dining and Recreation | $2,000 |
| Vacations | $2,000 |
| Gym Memberships | $1,700 |
| Gifts to Family | $295 |
| Video Streaming Service | $120 |
| TOTAL DISCRETIONARY SPENDING | $6,115 |

# They have now completed their cash flow breakdown:

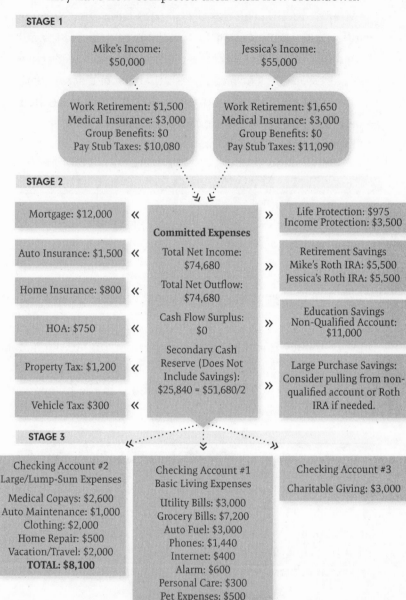

**STAGE 1**

Mike's Income:
$50,000

Jessica's Income:
$55,000

Work Retirement: $1,500
Medical Insurance: $3,000
Group Benefits: $0
Pay Stub Taxes: $10,080

Work Retirement: $1,650
Medical Insurance: $3,000
Group Benefits: $0
Pay Stub Taxes: $11,090

**STAGE 2**

Mortgage: $12,000 «

Auto Insurance: $1,500 «

Home Insurance: $800 «

HOA: $750 «

Property Tax: $1,200 «

Vehicle Tax: $300 «

**Committed Expenses**

Total Net Income:
$74,680

Total Net Outflow:
$74,680

Cash Flow Surplus:
$0

Secondary Cash
Reserve (Does Not
Include Savings):
$25,840 = $51,680/2

» Life Protection: $975
Income Protection: $3,500

» Retirement Savings
Mike's Roth IRA: $5,500
Jessica's Roth IRA: $5,500

» Education Savings
Non-Qualified Account:
$11,000

» Large Purchase Savings:
Consider pulling from non-
qualified account or Roth
IRA if needed.

**STAGE 3**

Checking Account #2
Large/Lump-Sum Expenses

Medical Copays: $2,600
Auto Maintenance: $1,000
Clothing: $2,000
Home Repair: $500
Vacation/Travel: $2,000
**TOTAL: $8,100**

Checking Account #1
Basic Living Expenses

Utility Bills: $3,000
Grocery Bills: $7,200
Auto Fuel: $3,000
Phones: $1,440
Internet: $400
Alarm: $600
Personal Care: $300
Pet Expenses: $500
Dining and Recreation: $2,000
Gym Memberships: $1,700
Gifts to Family: $295
Video Streaming: $120
**TOTAL: $20,555**

Checking Account #3

Charitable Giving: $3,000

Mike and Jessica have completed the most important steps in the foundation of the financial planning process. They have a game plan, and they have taken steps to help ensure that their game plan does not get thrown off course by unforeseen circumstances. Now comes the fun part. Instead of working tirelessly for the rest of their lives, they can choose to have their savings work for them.

## CHAPTER 9

# YOUR INVESTMENTS, YOUR MUSCLES: MAKING THE MOST OF WHAT YOU HAVE

*"If you mentally believe it will happen, your body is going to find a way to make it physically happen."*

**—GREG PLITT**

Once you know *where* to invest, the next important question is *how*. As stated in the beginning of the book, people often forget that every asset they own should have a purpose. Your investments are the muscles of your financial life. They can grow or shrink depending on how you use them.

In the gym you can control how frequently you target a particular muscle group, how much weight you add, and how many reps you complete. As your muscles grow, your ability to attempt new and more complex exercises improves. These new exercises can further enhance your physique, allowing you to mold your body and proportions toward your ideal image. In addition, your muscles can start working for you. They can burn calories at a faster rate, helping you to stay in shape without applying nearly as much effort.

This realization really hit home for me when I was watching one of Greg's early question-and-answer website videos. One of the members asked him how he was able to maintain such an incredible physique every year. Greg explained that maintaining is the easy part. It's getting started that is the major challenge.

The same is true in finance. There are so many different ways to invest, and while initially it may seem very chaotic and messy, the more properly structured your investment portfolios become, the more opportunities for growth you will discover. These various investment options can allow you to take greater advantage of tax and diversification opportunities as well as cost efficiencies available to you. Also, like your muscles working for you to burn calories, your investment portfolios will work for you through the profound effects of compound growth!

## COMPOUND GROWTH

Compound growth is the average rate of growth an investment experiences over a multiyear period. It considers not only the growth of the initial investment but also the growth of the investment's gains during that multiyear period.

To understand the effects of compound growth, let's analyze an example involving education savings. Assume that you have three different couples saving for their newborn child's college education expenses that will start in 18 years. Their goals are to reach $200,000 by year 18. The first couple starts saving $4,945 annually, and they put their savings into an investment portfolio that generates an average annual rate of return of 8 percent. They will invest just under $90,000 over the next 18 years and, in the end, reach their target goal!

Now imagine that the second couple decides to wait five years before making their first annual contribution. If their portfolio also achieves an annual 8 percent average rate of return, they will need to increase the annual savings level to $8,616. They will contribute a total of $112,008 toward education savings in order to reach their $200,000 goal.

Finally, the third couple waits nine years to begin saving for college. With the same assumed rate of return, they will need to save $14,830 annually, or a total of $133,470 toward their education goal. The first couple had to save $22,998 less than the second couple and $44,456 less than the third couple, all because they started their savings process earlier.

## EDUCATION SAVINGS COMPARISON CHART

| $4,945 INVESTED ANNUALLY STARTING AT AGE ONE | | $8,616 INVESTED ANNUALLY STARTING AT AGE SIX | | $14,830 INVESTED ANNUALLY STARTING AT AGE TEN | |
|---|---|---|---|---|---|
| Child's Age | Total Portfolio Value | Child's Age | Total Portfolio Value | Child's Age | Total Portfolio Value |
| 1 | $5,341 | 1 | $0 | 1 | $0 |
| 2 | $11,108 | 2 | $0 | 2 | $0 |
| 3 | $17,338 | 3 | $0 | 3 | $0 |
| 4 | $24,065 | 4 | $0 | 4 | $0 |
| 5 | $31,331 | 5 | $0 | 5 | $0 |
| 6 | $39,178 | 6 | $9,305 | 6 | $0 |
| 7 | $47,653 | 7 | $19,355 | 7 | $0 |
| 8 | $56,806 | 8 | $30,209 | 8 | $0 |

*table continued on next page*

| | | | | | |
|---|---|---|---|---|---|
| 9 | $66,691 | 9 | $41,931 | 9 | $0 |
| 10 | $77,367 | 10 | $54,590 | 10 | $16,016 |
| 11 | $88,897 | 11 | $68,293 | 11 | $33,314 |
| 12 | $101,349 | 12 | $83,029 | 12 | $51,996 |
| 13 | $114,798 | 13 | $98,977 | 13 | $72,172 |
| 14 | $129,322 | 14 | $116,200 | 14 | $93,962 |
| 15 | $145,009 | 15 | $134,802 | 15 | $117,495 |
| 16 | $161,950 | 16 | $154,891 | 16 | $142,911 |
| 17 | $180,246 | 17 | $176,587 | 17 | $170,360 |
| 18 | $200,007 | 18 | $200,020 | 18 | $200,006 |
| **TOTAL CON-TRIBU-TIONS** | **$89,010** | | **$112,008** | | **$133,470** |

This example of compound growth is even more significant when looking at retirement planning. Let's take the same three couples and assume that they all invest $5,000 annually at the beginning of each year, but begin the process at different ages:

## RETIREMENT SAVINGS COMPARISON CHART

| AGE | TOTAL PORTFOLIO VALUE | AGE | TOTAL PORTFOLIO VALUE | AGE | TOTAL PORTFOLIO VALUE |
|---|---|---|---|---|---|
| 30 | $5,400 | 30 | $0 | 30 | $0 |
| 31 | $11,232 | 31 | $0 | 31 | $0 |
| 32 | $17,531 | 32 | $0 | 32 | $0 |
| 33 | $24,333 | 33 | $0 | 33 | $0 |
| 34 | $31,680 | 34 | $0 | 34 | $0 |
| 35 | $39,614 | 35 | $5,400 | 35 | $0 |
| 36 | $48,183 | 36 | $11,232 | 36 | $0 |
| 37 | $57,438 | 37 | $17,531 | 37 | $0 |
| 38 | $67,433 | 38 | $24,333 | 38 | $0 |

| | | | | | |
|---|---|---|---|---|---|
| 39 | $78,227 | 39 | $31,680 | 39 | $0 |
| 40 | $89,886 | 40 | $39,614 | 40 | $5,400 |
| 41 | $102,476 | 41 | $48,183 | 41 | $11,232 |
| 42 | $116,075 | 42 | $57,438 | 42 | $17,531 |
| 43 | $130,761 | 43 | $67,433 | 43 | $24,333 |
| 44 | $146,621 | 44 | $78,227 | 44 | $31,680 |
| 45 | $163,751 | 45 | $89,886 | 45 | $39,614 |
| 46 | $182,251 | 46 | $102,476 | 46 | $48,183 |
| 47 | $202,231 | 47 | $116,075 | 47 | $57,438 |
| 48 | $223,810 | 48 | $130,761 | 48 | $67,433 |
| 49 | $247,115 | 49 | $146,621 | 49 | $78,227 |
| 50 | $272,284 | 50 | $163,751 | 50 | $89,886 |
| 51 | $299,466 | 51 | $182,251 | 51 | $102,476 |
| 52 | $328,824 | 52 | $202,231 | 52 | $116,075 |
| 53 | $360,530 | 53 | $223,810 | 53 | $130,761 |
| 54 | $394,772 | 54 | $247,115 | 54 | $146,621 |
| 55 | $431,754 | 55 | $272,284 | 55 | $163,751 |
| 56 | $471,694 | 56 | $299,466 | 56 | $182,251 |
| 57 | $514,830 | 57 | $328,824 | 57 | $202,231 |
| 58 | $561,416 | 58 | $360,530 | 58 | $223,810 |
| 59 | $611,729 | 59 | $394,772 | 59 | $247,115 |
| 60 | $666,068 | 60 | $431,754 | 60 | $272,284 |
| 61 | $724,753 | 61 | $471,694 | 61 | $299,466 |
| 62 | $788,133 | 62 | $514,830 | 62 | $328,824 |
| 63 | $856,584 | 63 | $561,416 | 63 | $360,530 |
| 64 | $930,511 | 64 | $611,729 | 64 | $394,772 |
| 65 | $1,010,352 | 65 | $666,068 | 65 | $431,754 |
| TOTAL CONTRIBUTIONS | $180,000 | | $155,000 | | $130,000 |

By starting their savings at age 30, the first couple will have over $1,000,000 saved for retirement by age 65, while the couple that waited until age 40 to start saving will have less than $432,000. The first couple's additional savings of $50,000 over the first 10 years resulted in a surge in their portfolio that more than doubled their results. That is the effect of compound growth and the reason that it is so essential to begin saving for your future goals as soon as possible. Make your investments work for you!

## INVESTMENT ALLOCATION

While I hope that these charts motivate you, it is also important to acknowledge that investing without purpose and understanding may lead to confusion. You may start to second-guess your decisions and lose sight of why you started investing in the first place. The emotional roller coaster of investing can drive some people to develop habits that sabotage their long-term planning goals and savings strategies.

Investment planning or investment allocation is where the emotion of comprehensive financial planning really starts to take hold. Just as systematic saving is vital to achieve your long-term financial goals, investment allocation also plays a critical role. There are hundreds of books that provide advice on investment options and strategies. You can invest in stocks, bonds, precious metals, mutual funds, exchange-traded funds, immediate annuities, CDs, money market accounts, and more. If you want to get more complex, you can look at alternative investments vehicles like real estate investment trusts (REITs), options, hedge funds, and private equity investments.

Each investment category comes with its own list of sub-categories. Stocks can be broken down into large-cap, mid-cap, small-cap, international, emerging markets, real estate, and more. They can further be split into value-based, growth-based, or a blend of the two. Bonds can be purchased as treasury, municipal, corporate, international, and more. Annuities can be fixed, variable, immediate, or indexed. The list of available investment options only seems to grow as technology improves. Feeling overwhelmed yet?

Determining the best investment strategy can be so intimidating that almost any sane person would quit as soon as they started researching all the options. What makes investment allocation in today's world even more challenging is that we live in an era where information and advice are easily accessible. If you want to learn about something, all you need to do is pull out your smartphone and start researching online. Thousands of articles sit at the ready. Bookshelves stand littered with self-help books that promise to teach you how to invest like a professional.

This abundance of information exists in finance, in fitness, and in almost any other profession. You don't need to hire a plumber; just watch the YouTube video. You don't need to go see the doctor; you can diagnose your own condition using online sites like WebMD. Want to learn how to play the guitar or piano? Well, there's an app for that. Having trouble with your diet? Don't worry—an article on a nutrition site says it has all of the answers.

While today we find that information is easily and abundantly accessible, there are other truths that we need to recognize. As a society, people have become less handy around the house than in previous decades. We are becoming more obese. Many people today are in worse financial shape than their parents and grandparents.

Why are we so much worse at caring for our physical and financial health today, even with all of this information available? I believe the answer can be summed up in one common phrase: *analysis paralysis*. In decision-making, when we are given too many options, our fight-or-flight instincts take over and we often choose flight. Ignorance and denial are much easier to manage subconsciously than seeking professional help and being forced to make a decision. Trying to do all the research and analysis on our own is even harder!

Remember how I felt the first time I visited Greg's website and discovered over 600 variations of exercises? I was intimidated, and my mind immediately started telling me that I had neither the time nor the energy to begin absorbing all of the information. I wanted to log off and stay ignorant, but Greg had incorporated two very important features into his site that helped me to hang on. These two features are direction and options.

Let's start with direction. On his site, Greg laid out an easy-to-understand process for how to approach fitness training and working out. He called it his 90-Day Transformation Calendar. The calendar clearly identifies what muscle groups or cardio exercises members should target each day. It provides pre-written workouts inside of each muscle group and video tutorials explaining how to properly do each exercise. This program and the recommended workouts were what Greg personally used to acquire his incredible physique. Members know that they are getting the real deal and not a new gimmick workout program.

The direction Greg provided gives clarity to what members need to do, but what makes the site even more attractive is that members are given multiple options when it comes to exercises and workouts. They can choose different variations of chest or arm workouts. They can find exercises that fit their physical abilities and their target goals. Beginners can choose basic exercises, while more advanced members can integrate more challenging ones into their daily workouts. Members are never restricted to using just one set approach.

This concept may sound very simple, but think of the exercise or diet programs that you may have tried in the past. Did they restrict you to only certain food groups or certain repeated exercises? If so, chances are that you, like me, gave them a try but quit after some short period of time. Our lives are always evolving. We are always learning. What works well today may be outdated tomorrow. Any program that does not have the capability to change and evolve is destined to fail.

So let's go back to the understanding that there are many different investment vehicles available in the world today. I could attempt to list the benefits and drawbacks of each one, and my efforts would likely result in nearly doubling the size of this book—but the information alone would only skim the surface of how these vehicles work and which may be best for you and your family.

Every family's situation and goals are different. There is not one investment vehicle or investment strategy that is better than all of the others, though there are plenty of television and radio talking heads who will say that their way is the only way to go. Remember, those media personalities don't know you, and they don't know your family. They don't know your goals. Although many of them may have very good intentions, restricting yourself and your family to one investment approach could result in lost opportunities and careless mistakes.

While it is important to make sure that you do not restrict your investment philosophy to one set approach, there are a few key aspects of investment planning that clients always should consider when developing their investment portfolios.

## DIVERSIFICATION

The first aspect is diversification. When you diversify a portfolio, you spread the risk of your investments across multiple sectors of the market with the understanding that these sectors are not fully correlated to one another. It is nearly impossible to accurately time the market every year, and no one sector is always the best or worst performer. For example, look at the best and worst performing sectors of the market from 1997 to 2016.[1]

### BEST AND WORST PERFORMING SECTORS

| YEAR | BEST PERFORMING | WORST PERFORMING |
|------|-----------------|------------------|
| 2016 | Small/Mid-Cap | Cash |
| 2015 | Large-Cap Growth | Commodities |
| 2014 | Real Estate | Commodities |
| 2013 | Small/Mid-Cap | Commodities |
| 2012 | Real Estate (REITs) | Commodities |
| 2011 | Bonds | Commodities |
| 2010 | Real Estate (REITs) | Cash |
| 2009 | Large-Cap Growth | Cash |
| 2008 | Global Bonds | International |
| 2007 | Commodities | Real Estate (REITs) |
| 2006 | Real Estate (REITs) | Commodities |
| 2005 | Commodities | Global Bonds |
| 2004 | Real Estate (REITs) | Cash |
| 2003 | Small/Mid-Cap | Cash |

---

1 Massachusetts Financial Services Company. Disciplined Diversification® brochure. www.mfs.com/wps/FileServerServlet?articleId=templatedata/internet/file/data/sales_tools/mfsp_20yrsa_fly&servletCommand=default. Accessed November 1, 2017.

| 2002 | Commodities | Large-Cap Growth |
| 2001 | Real Estate (REITs) | International |
| 2000 | Commodities | Large-Cap Growth |
| 1999 | Large-Cap Growth | Real Estate (REITs) |
| 1998 | Large-Cap Growth | Commodities |
| 1997 | Large-Cap Value | Commodities |

See any pattern? The reality is that there is no way to tell what the future will hold when it comes to best and worst performing sectors. One sector can be the best performer one year and the worst performer the next. Trying to time the market and consistently pick the best sectors is a gamble, one that for many families does not pay off.

Diversifying your investment portfolio helps to avoid the risk of having all your eggs in one basket. By adding multiple sectors of the market into your portfolio, you reduce the risk of having one sector's poor performance cause serious harm to your investment returns and, consequently, to your long-term investment goals.

When discussing diversification, financial advisors often like to focus on something called your *standard deviation*. Standard deviation helps determine the volatility associated with an investment. Simply put, it helps you determine how likely it is that the portfolio will stray from its mean or average rate of return. A good advisor will make sure that each of your investment accounts is allocated to match its designated time horizons and return goals. He or she will also confirm that each portfolio's standard deviation falls within a risk range that you are willing to accept.

Going back to the investment accounts listed on the net worth statement in chapter 3, I would suggest the following risk profiles:

| TIME HORIZON | RETURN RANGE | RISK PROFILE |
|---|---|---|
| Less than three years | 0%–3% | Fixed Income/Conservative |
| Two to five years | 2%–4% | Conservative/Mod. Conservative |
| Five to ten years | 4%–6% | Moderate/Moderate Aggressive |
| Ten-plus years | 7%–10% | Moderate Aggressive/Aggressive |

Trying to determine what vehicles to use to invest—as well as how to allocate an appropriate ratio of stock and fixed income investments—can be very complicated and stressful. You and your spouse will need to determine whether you want to do the research yourselves or seek the professional guidance of a management tool or financial planner. Using a fitness analogy, do you want to just look in the mirror and determine your own workout routine based on your level of understanding, or do you think the professional help of a fitness trainer would more accurately pinpoint your areas of weakness and opportunity?

Doing nothing should never be an option, yet it is the option many people unknowingly take. When I first meet with potential clients, I ask how they chose the investments in their retirement plans. Answers often include picking funds at random, seeing which one was the best performer last year and selecting it, or, more commonly, having no idea what the investments are. They don't know if their investments are in line with their goals and time horizons. They are not in control.

Don't allow ignorance to sabotage your financial future! Identify your investment accounts, determine their risk profiles and time horizons, and allocate them accordingly. If you're not sure how to do it, seek professional guidance. Don't go at it blind.

## SYSTEMATIC REBALANCING

Once you have diversified your investment portfolio, you must then make sure that the portfolio is monitored and rebalanced. Markets are constantly shifting. You have to be aware of those shifts and make changes to your portfolio in response to them. You have probably heard the old saying "Buy low, sell high." The concept seems simple. When an investment has a low value, you should buy more of it. Conversely, when an investment has a high value, you should lock in your gains and sell it.

While the concept is somewhat easy to understand, the harsh reality is that it completely goes against the way our brains are wired. We want more of whatever is giving us the most satisfaction or seems to be performing the best. Greg gave a great example of this understanding in the fitness world. He explained that when most guys go to the gym, they often want to work on their chest or bicep muscles because those are usually the most visible and easiest to show off. The problem comes when those same guys take off their shirts. They have a rock-solid chest and bulging biceps, but down below is a big round belly that looks like it hasn't seen a sit-up in years. That image of physical fitness rapidly fades as the belly becomes the focal point of the person's physique.

To address this issue, Greg developed a workout program that focuses on shifting daily workouts to different muscle groups. For example, day one may be cardio, with chest on day two, back on day three, shoulders on day four, arms on day five, cardio or a full body workout on day six, and legs on day seven. The rotation constantly changes. It allows members to give their recently exercised muscles time to rest. It also forces members to concentrate their future workouts on muscles or cardio activities that target their weaker areas. Using Greg's program, members not only can confidently show off their chests and biceps, but also proudly know that every part of their body is in prime shape. They have the full package!

The same logic applies in financial planning. Make sure that you systematically rebalance your investment portfolio. Take emotion out of the picture. Don't get caught saying, "Well, I am going to wait until after I have recovered my losses before I sell this stock," or "I have had my money in this fund for years and it has done incredibly well! I am going to keep my money here and keep riding the wave up." These two mindsets often lead to problems. Give purpose to every investment that you have, and stick to your game plan.

In addition, avoid trying to "time the market." Pulling your investments out of the market because you are worried about a potential correction or recession could result in a significant long-term negative impact to your investment portfolio. One of the most eye-opening statistics I've seen in my career as an advisor is a chart that shows the impact of missing just a few days of strong upward growth in the market.[2] For example, if you had invested money into the S&P 500 index back in 1996 and allowed it to sit there for 20 years, your average rate of return would have been about 8.19 percent over the 20-year period. Look at the difference in average return if you missed between 5 and 60 of the best performing days during that 20-year period:

2 Ryan Vlastelica. "Think You Can Time the Stock Market? Look at This Chart First." MarketWatch, December 11, 2017. https://www.marketwatch.com/story/think-you-can-time-the-stock-market-look-at-this-chart-first-2017-12-08. Accessed November 1, 2018.

| MISSED # OF BEST DAYS | AVERAGE RATE OF RETURN |
| --- | --- |
| Fully Invested | 8.19% |
| 5 Best Days | 5.99% |
| 10 Best Days | 4.00% |
| 15 Best Days | 2.74% |
| 20 Best Days | 1.57% |
| 30 Best Days | -0.51% |
| 40 Best Days | -2.42% |
| 50 Best Days | -3.71% |
| 60 Best Days | -5.76% |

Missing just 60 days in a 20-year period changed the average rate of return over that period from 8.19 to -5.76 percent. Trying to time the market is rarely worth the risk. Remember the purpose behind each portfolio and its time horizon. Long-term investments can ride out volatility!

## LIQUIDITY

I stated earlier that one of my favorite *F* words is *flexibility*. Liquidity is a great tool to use to help ensure flexibility with your overall investment portfolio. According to the online resource *Investopedia*, liquidity describes the degree to which an asset can be quickly bought or sold in the market without affecting the asset's price.

Before purchasing any investment, you will want to research what restrictions exist for that particular investment. Certain market investments—including stocks, ETFs, and mutual funds—are very liquid, meaning that you can get access to the cash from these investments within a week if needed. Other investments—including certain annuities, REITs, CDs, individual bonds, and permanent cash value life insurance policies—can be extremely illiquid, in some cases tying up your money with heavy penalties for 10 years or longer. Illiquid investment vehicles can certainly play a positive role in a family's overall investment portfolio, but before committing to any illiquid product, make sure that both you and your spouse have a very clear understanding of how it works, its purpose, and what the early withdrawal penalties are. Don't get stuck!

## COST EFFICIENCY

Cost efficiency in investment planning, and more broadly in overall financial planning, is an immensely important area of focus for all families. It is important not only from a financial standpoint, but also from a psychological point of view. Cost efficiency involves examining your investment accounts to identify all fees and expenses associated with the accounts. These fees could be administrative, managerial, custodial, and/or other.

I stated earlier that people have access to more information today than ever before, yet, as a society, we are often moving in the wrong direction. Many people are in worse physical and financial shape than their parents and grandparents. Part of this degrading of financial and physical wellness has to do with information overload, but I believe the other, more significant part has to do with a particular mindset: the desire to get as much as possible for free.

In today's technology-driven society, we are constantly bombarded with messaging that states that if you pay for something, then someone is taking advantage of you. Why pay to see the doctor, the dentist, the mechanic, the plumber, the fitness trainer, the CPA, or the financial advisor? After all, you can get all of your questions answered online. You can buy almost anything you want online. Why pay someone to manage a mutual fund or an investment portfolio? You can just pick some extremely low-cost passive index funds and then create and manage your own portfolio.

Sounds easy, right? The reality is that while the basics of these decision topics are easy to understand, the more complex components can quickly lead to difficult questions and confusion. There is a reason that professionals exist. What happens when you file your taxes and do not understand a certain deduction? What happens when you feel sick, but you're unsure about the diagnosis and remedy for your symptoms listed on a group blog? What happens when you watch a YouTube video on how to rewire your backyard lights, but after all is done, the lights don't work?

In these scenarios, you are forced to make one of three choices. You can seek out the professional help of an expert, continue to research the problem on your own with the hope that you will eventually find a solution, or give up on the project. Most people choose option three. They tell themselves, "If I can't fix the lights, then I'll just let them stay broken. If I can't figure out why I am feeling sick, then I'll just hope that it eventually goes away. If I don't understand the deduction, then I'll just not include it."

In finance, a dislike of fees is one reason people avoid making a decision. The idea of paying money in order to make money seems counterintuitive. We are constantly told that there is a cheaper investment option. We are told to skip getting a human advisor and to just use the website. Many discount financial services companies over the past decade appear to have entered into an all-out war with one another over who can be the leading low-cost provider.

While these reductions in management fees and increased transparency have certainly helped consumers, they have also led to a minimalistic approach to financial advice. The old phrase "You get what you pay for" is becoming more evident every year. Young families searching for help with questions related to how certain investment vehicles work or where they should save are being redirected to a website, a brochure, or an online article. In some cases, they are being stopped at the door. Certain full-service advisory-based firms are setting minimum investment thresholds as high as $250,000 for a family to even speak to an advisor. These minimums and restrictions are forcing families to go it alone, and, after realizing how much there is to digest, many families choose option three and throw up their hands.

A better way to explain this psychological impact is to use a personal fitness analogy. This analogy struck me one day when I was doing one of Greg's recommended chest exercises. It was a simple exercise: push-ups. I had been doing push-ups for as long as I could remember, and the components of a proper push-up seemed very obvious. I would place my body on the floor, parallel with the ground, and then push my body up until my arms were fully extended. I would then go down until my arms came to a 90-degree angle.

This particular day, I noticed that Greg's description of the workout was "Shoulder-Width Push-Ups." I had done this exercise at least 20 times, incorrectly. My hands were too wide apart.

So I watched a short tutorial video on the site and then adjusted my hands, moving them closer together so that they were just shoulder width apart. The next push-up made me feel like I had never completed a push-up in my life. The new shoulder-width push-up hit a completely different set of chest and tricep muscles. It was much more intense and efficient than my original wide-grip style.

During my initial months of working out, I did not use Greg's recommended correct form when doing push-ups—but I still did some form of a push-up and got stronger. I learned through trial and error. I did not try any exercises that were beyond my comfort zone or that put my body at risk. Instead, I used the professional advice that was provided to me and, in time, discovered ways to improve my exercises and overall workout program.

This understanding can very easily apply to finance. If you wait to research all of your investment options to determine the absolute most cost-efficient approach, you may very quickly discover that your search is endless, and the time that you have spent researching option after option is now all lost. You may also get so frustrated in your search that you give up and do nothing. Here is where you need to remember the following: High fees equal bad form, but no form is even worse!

Don't sacrifice your entire investment planning strategy just because of administrative or management fees. Yes, fees will diminish your returns, but study after study has shown that families that pay for investment advice and comprehensive planning advice perform better overall on their long-term investments and savings strategies than families that try to do it all on their own.

According to Mike Eklund of NerdWallet, "Vanguard released a paper in 2014 that found that a financial advisor can add as much as 3 percent of value in net portfolio returns per year through smart financial decisions. A study by Morningstar found that advice from a financial planner can add 29 percent more wealth through retirement. And a recent study by John Hancock Retirement Plan Services found that 70 percent of those who work with a financial advisor or planner are on track or ahead in saving for retirement, compared with 33 percent of those not working with an advisor."[3] It is possible that your advisor may not select the absolute best funds, but just like my push-ups, having a good strategy that helps you to improve and grow is far better than avoiding any decision and waiting to see what happens.

When creating an investment allocation, make sure to focus on proper diversification, systematic rebalancing, and a high level of liquidity. With these in place, your investment portfolio should have the ability to adjust to new and more cost-efficient investing opportunities in the future. Don't get stuck. Be prepared to make the hard choice on going it alone or seeking professional help. Doing nothing should never be one of your options!

---

3 Mike Eklund. "Are Financial Advisors Worth the Fee?" *Christian Science Monitor*, February 18, 2016. https://www.csmonitor.com/Business/Saving-Money/2016/0218/Are-financial-advisors-worth-the-fee. Accessed March 14, 2018.

**CHAPTER 10**

# FINDING THE RIGHT FINANCIAL PLANNER

*"All you have is today. Today is all you've got. Do you make the most of today? Do you make today remembered?"*

**—GREG PLITT**

Now you and your spouse need to make a critical decision. You need to carefully consider and determine whether you both have the time, the desire, the knowledge, and the energy to accomplish the following:

- Identify all of your assets and liabilities to create a detailed net worth statement, highlighting both the purpose and the estimated ranges of return for your assets as well as the interest rates for your liabilities.

- Determine a strategy to eliminate any high-interest consumer debt.

- Identify and segment your incomes and expenses to generate a cash flow statement that accurately reflects your current financial situation, placing your future committed goals above your present discretionary wants.

- Determine an appropriate cash reserve target and how best to allocate your available cash reserves.

- Address your life protection needs and determine the most appropriate types of policies to cover those needs.

- Address your income protection needs and determine the most appropriate types of policies to cover those needs.

- Address your pre-death and post-death estate planning needs and make sure that all of your investment account and insurance policy beneficiary designations are updated to reflect the language of your estate documents.

- Identify the tax savings vehicles you have available, both in and outside of work, and determine which of these vehicles are the most appropriate to maximize tax efficiency now and in retirement.

- Examine your available work retirement and medical benefits to determine whether you are fully utilizing these benefits to reach your goals.

- Develop a strategy to achieve your short-term major expense goals, which may include a new home purchase, a home refinance, and/or a car purchase.

- Determine what savings levels you need to establish in order to achieve your mid- and long-term financial planning goals. These goals may include family planning, education planning, and retirement planning.

- Examine your personal and spousal Social Security benefits to determine how to maximize these benefits in retirement.

- Examine your investment account asset allocations to determine whether they are properly diversified and allocated to have a risk profile that matches their purpose and time horizon.

- Track and rebalance your investment portfolios on a periodic basis.

The list continues, but if just reading all of these financial planning responsibilities makes you feel overwhelmed and stressed, seek the guidance of a financial planner who can provide comprehensive advice. I emphasize the word *comprehensive*. In today's financial environment, almost anyone can call themselves a "financial advisor." The title has lost its value and its meaning. People who have little to no financial experience or expertise can slap on the *advisor* label simply because they work at the local bank or sit behind a desk at the insurance company's call center. When you are ready to seek help, be sure to do your homework and make the right decision the first time.

When searching for a financial planner, focus on both the profession and the person. Starting with the profession, it is important to understand that there are many different types of financial advisors. There are investment advisors, tax advisors, estate planners, mortgage brokers, real estate agents, insurance agents, debt advisors, and even money coaches. Each type of advisor has his or her own unique specialties and credentials. Trying to find a specialist in each one of these fields can be overwhelming and cost prohibitive. This is why I suggest that you hire a financial planner who has the qualifications to provide comprehensive guidance.

This type of planner is not necessarily an expert in each of the particular fields mentioned above. Instead, he or she should be an expert at both understanding your family's financial situation and personal goals and utilizing different professionals to help you achieve those goals. The financial planner becomes the center axel in a wheelhouse of advice.

## FINANCIAL PLANNER'S WHEELHOUSE OF COMPREHENSIVE ADVICE

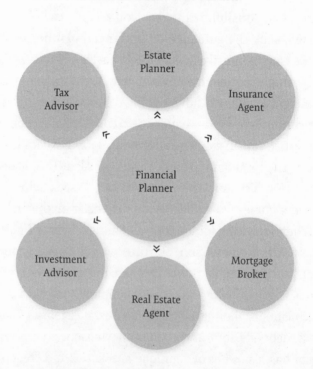

The complexity of financial planning decisions simplifies when you have just one person to contact rather than six. So now the question becomes, How do you find this one person, especially in a world where so many people claim that they have all of the answers? Consider the following key steps before and during the interview process.

## BASICS AND CREDENTIALS

Visit https://brokercheck.finra.org to determine whether any disclosures or complaints have been filed against the advisor.

Confirm that the advisor has completed the Series 7 Exam. The Series 7 Exam, or the General Securities Representative Qualification Exam (GS), measures the degree to which an advisor possesses the knowledge needed to perform the critical functions of a general securities representative, including sales of corporate securities, municipal securities, investment company securities, variable annuities, direct participation programs, options, and government securities.[1]

Confirm that the advisor has completed the Series 66 Exam. The Series 66 Exam, or the NASAA Uniform Combined State Law Exam, is designed to qualify candidates as both securities agents and investment advisor representatives.[2]

Confirm that the advisor has the appropriate life and income producer or agent licenses to be able to offer individual insurance policies in your state of residence.

There are many different credentials that can be listed next to an advisor's name. Some are easy to acquire while others are extremely difficult. When seeking comprehensive guidance, look for an advisor who is a CERTIFIED FINANCIAL PLANNER™ (CFP®)

---

1 Financial Industry Regulatory Authority. Series 7 Exam: General Securities Representative Exam (GS). www.finra.org/industry/series7. Accessed November 1, 2017.
2 Wikipedia. "Uniform Combined State Law Exam." www.wikipedia.org/wiki/uniform_Combined_State_Law_Exam. Accessed November 1, 2017.

or Chartered Financial Consultant® (ChFC®). These designations have a very strong focus on holistic financial planning. If you are strictly seeking investment advice, search for an advisor who is a Chartered Financial Analyst® (CFA).

## TIME

Confirm that the advisor has worked in the financial services industry for at least four years. The initial three years of an advisor's career are the most likely period where the advisor may choose to call it quits and switch to another profession. If possible, try to find an advisor that has at least a decade's worth of experience.

Ask whether you will be assigned to a specific advisor or to a sub-level advisor. One of the best ways to get a sense of how much time the advisor is likely to dedicate to your family is to ask the advisor how many client groups he or she currently has under management. If the advisor says 150 to 200, then there is a good possibility that the advisor will have the available time to give you high-quality service. If the number is well above 300, then ask if you will be working directly with the advisor or someone else on the team. With a client pool of that size, you could become just a number.

## AGE

While you can't directly ask the advisor's age, it is something you certainly want to consider. Older advisors (in their 50s or beyond) may have a great deal more experience, but you have to consider their professional game plan as well. Do they plan to retire in the next 10 to 15 years? What is their contingency plan when they leave the industry or if something should happen to them? You may not want to rebuild a planning relationship with a newly assigned advisor every 10 years.

## CLIENT SATISFACTION

Determine whether the advisor has any type of client satisfaction score. If yes, make sure to ask about the score and how it was created. If you discover that the advisor's client satisfaction level is under 80 percent, you might consider seeking out another professional. Low scores often result from poor response times, including callbacks and email replies. In my experience, responsiveness and transparency by the advisor are the leading indicators of client satisfaction.

## FIDUCIARY ADVICE

Confirm that the advisor is required to act in your best interest or, more specifically, as a fiduciary when providing investment or comprehensive planning advice. Many clients are under the assumption that their advisors are automatically required to provide fiduciary advice. This is not the case. Some advisors are held to a much lower "suitability" standard, which states that their recommendations only need to be suitable and not necessarily in the client's best interest.

## COMPENSATION

Determine how the advisor is compensated. One great gut check when you interview potential advisors is to see whether they share how they are compensated before you have to ask. This is usually done in the opening interview or introductory phone call. Advisors should always keep their fees as transparent as possible. There are three different modes of compensation for an advisor: fee only, fee based, or commission based.

Fee-only advisors often work in a strictly advisory, hands-off capacity. They develop financial plans that can provide either broad or specific recommendations on how clients should address their various planning needs and goals. Once the recommendations are made, it is then the responsibility of the client to complete the recommendations. The client often needs to set up the investment accounts, place the recommended trades, and research and purchase the recommended insurance policies on their own. Fee-only advisors can be very helpful for individuals who want to do as much as possible on their own, but would like some guidance along the way.

Fee-based advisors usually charge a percentage fee on the assets that are placed under their management. They can also provide comprehensive financial planning advice and help clients implement that advice, but as the portfolio grows, their compensation also grows. Once the portfolio reaches a certain size, clients may have the ability to negotiate down the management expense being charged. I suggest that clients look at this type of relationship as a "growing together" approach with their advisor.

Commission-based advisors typically focus on making and implementing investment recommendations and receive commissions on the investment products that you purchase through them. These commissions could be trading fees on stock transactions inside of a brokerage account, insurance premiums on new life or disability insurance policies, or up-front "loads" or charges on investment vehicles like REITs or immediate annuities. These fees are sometimes difficult to determine or embedded in the structure of the product.

So how do you determine which compensation structure is best? Try to find a financial planner who can work in all three categories, without being limited in the type or scope of advice that he or she can provide. If your advisor can work with you to develop a financial plan for your unique needs for a fixed fee, then you likely have someone who can help you address all of your financial goals. If the advisor can also help you set up the investment vehicles and insurance policies needed to implement the financial plan, then you have the added benefit of being able to choose whether you want the advisor's help to complete your plan's recommendations or will try to do it all on your own.

## REALISTIC EXPECTATIONS

When you consider fees, make sure that you have a very real understanding of how much you are paying for advice and an advisory relationship. Some advisory programs provide advice for as little as 0.3 percent of the investment portfolio value. This means that if you have $50,000 invested with the company, they will charge you about $150 per year to provide advice. Keep in mind that the full $150 is not going to the advisor. Portions of the fee go toward the company, compliance costs, marketing expenses, administrative expenses, staffing expenses, and much more. In reality, the advisor may receive about 40 percent of the fees charged. In this example, that would be about $60 for the year.

How many hours would you dedicate toward a client if your compensation for the year was $60? In my experience, the most basic financial plans require a minimum of about five hours to develop, not including meeting times or unscheduled calls. If we assume that the client requires just five hours of service annually, the advisor would be making an hourly gross income of $12.

How long do you anticipate that advisor will stay in the

industry? How much time do you anticipate he or she will dedicate to you and your family in future years after the assets have arrived? It is important to have realistic expectations of what quality and quantity of service you will receive after entering into any financial planning relationship. In today's world, it is more evident than ever before that you truly do get what you pay for.

When discussing compensation and fee structures with an advisor, see if she will give you a menu of services that outlines not only how she will be compensated but also what you will get for the fees you are charged. For asset management, advisors typically charge a fee starting in the 1 percent to 1.5 percent range. As the portfolio grows, that fee can be negotiated downward. Regarding comprehensive financial planning fees, they can vary widely based on the state where the advisor is located as well as the overall complexity of the plan. The advisor should have a fee guide that helps explain how the fees are determined. The more information the advisor can provide, the more clarity you will have in making your decision.

### RELATIONSHIP AND RESPECT

Finally, and probably most importantly, make sure that the advisor you select demonstrates the ethical and moral standards that you would expect of a professional—or any person, for that matter. Knowledge and experience are both valuable, but there is nothing more demoralizing than working with a professional who makes you feel unimportant or unwanted.

I witnessed a great example of the importance of respect and relationship when I first examined Greg's website. I discovered that people did not join Greg's site just for the exercises. There were plenty of other sites that offered workout programs and exercise routines, and many of them were even free!

The reason that so many people joined Greg's website and stayed was because they could relate to Greg, and he could relate to them. He would give them honest advice. He wouldn't just tell them what they wanted to hear. He kept things transparent. It didn't matter if any particular member was a Fortune 500 CEO or a high school teacher. Greg treated all individuals with the same level of compassion and respect. He didn't judge his site members, but he encouraged them to judge themselves and to ask if they truly were sticking to their commitments and goals. He didn't accept excuses, but he also didn't reject people who had made them and were trying to get back on track. He rejoiced with members when they accomplished their goals, and empathized when they experienced setbacks. His members knew that he wholeheartedly cared about them and wanted them to succeed.

When you search for a financial planner to help you achieve your personal and family goals, make sure that you experience the same type of relationship. Find someone who is willing to help you and who shares the same passion in seeing you achieve your goals and stick to your commitments. There are inevitably going to be some minor mistakes made by both you and the advisor along the way, but if the passion and respect are there, together you will achieve great things!

## CHAPTER 11

# OWNING
# THE DASH

*"Life is Yes. Excuses create Nos. We eliminate the
excuses through hard work, finding the meaning in
the dash. Own it! Work for it! Fight for it!"*

**—GREG PLITT**

I have learned over the years that success in reaching any goal
in life has far more to do with how we view our goals than with
statistics or minor details. I have made mistakes in my years as a
husband, a father, and a financial advisor, and I will likely make
more in the years to come, but the passion to constantly improve
myself and care for my family and clients will never fade.

There will always be setbacks in your life, and the things that
you care for most will both drive you and hinder you. Words like
*tomorrow* and *family* will encourage you to rise to the occasion, but
you will also use these same words as excuses for bad behavior.

You will say to yourself, "I don't have time to do it today. I'll take care of it tomorrow," or "I plan to get to work on that as soon as I can, but my family commitments right now are getting in the way."

Remember that every passion in your life can both drive you and depress you. It all depends on how you choose to approach it. Make sure that you keep an open mind and that you also constantly find the meaning in what you do to support yourself and your family.

My cousin realized early in life that he had a limited period of time to accomplish his hopes and dreams. Greg cherished every day and lived each day to its fullest. As he grew into a successful model, fitness coach, and business entrepreneur, he emphasized to his fans the importance of holding yourself accountable to your dreams. Greg once said, "They say dreams are things that you see when you are sleeping. I say dreams are things that keep you from sleeping because you can't wait to become them!" He went on to explain that we are either living our dreams or living our fears. The question is, Which are you giving the most time to?

Remember Greg's definition of "the dash": It is the time that you are given on this earth to reach your full potential, achieve your dreams, and build a positive legacy that you can pass on to others. There is truly nothing out there stopping you, except for yourself. The journey may sometimes be difficult, but the pain that you feel will be temporary. The pride that you feel will be forever. Greg constantly reminded his fans, "When you follow through on things in life, you achieve the confidence, the mentality, that anything is possible. No regrets. No wonders of 'what if.' Just excited for what can be."

So don't give up on your dreams! Work with your family as

a team. Take advantage of professional support when you need it. Do what you must to make your dreams a reality with no excuses to hold you back. Find the meaning in your dash—and own it!

# APPENDIX: PLANNING DOCUMENTS

## Your Planning Checklist

### NET WORTH AND CASH FLOW

_____ Develop a net worth statement

_____ Develop a cash flow statement

_____ Pay off all consumer liabilities with interest rates above 4%

### PROTECTION

_____ Build an efficient cash reserve

_____ Address life protection needs

_____ Address income protection needs

_____ Address estate planning needs

    _____ Create basic wills

    _____ Create health care directives

    _____ Create power of attorney documents

    _____ Identify an executor and a guardian(s)

    _____ Confirm account and insurance policy beneficiary designations

    _____ Determine whether you wish to set up a revocable living trust

## TAX AND INVESTMENT STRATEGIES

_____ Develop a tax-efficient savings strategy using the Tax Control Triangle approach

_____ Rebalance investment account portfolios to match risk tolerance and time horizons

_____ Set up systems to have investment portfolios rebalanced periodically

_____ Other:

_____ Other:

## POTENTIAL MAJOR PURCHASE PLANNING GOALS

_____ Purchase a car

_____ Purchase a home

_____ Other:

_____ Other:

## LONG-TERM PLANNING GOALS

_____ Plan for retirement

_____ Plan for college education

_____ Other:

_____ Other:

# Your Net Worth

| ASSETS | | | |
|---|---|---|---|
| TYPE | AMOUNT | EST. RATE OF RETURN | PURPOSE |
| Cash Reserve Investments (e.g., checking, savings, money market, CDs, etc.) | | | |
| | $ | | |
| | $ | | |
| | $ | | |
| | $ | | |
| Work Retirement Plans (e.g., 401(k), 403(b), 457, cash balance pension, etc.) | | | |
| | $ | | |
| | $ | | |
| Investment Accounts Outside of Work (e.g., IRA, Roth IRA, 529, brokerage account, etc.) | | | |
| | $ | | |
| | $ | | |
| | $ | | |
| | $ | | |
| | $ | | |
| Personal Assets (e.g., house, car, investment property, personal property, etc.) | | | |
| | $ | | |
| | $ | | |
| | $ | | |
| | $ | | |
| TOTAL ASSETS | $ | | |

*table continued on next page*

| LIABILITIES | | |
| --- | --- | --- |
| TYPE | AMOUNT | INTEREST CHARGED |
| | $ | |
| | $ | |
| | $ | |
| | $ | |
| TOTAL LIABILITIES | $ | |
| NET WORTH | $_____ =<br>Total Assets ($_____) – Total Liabilities ($_____) | |

# Your Annual Cash Flow

| ANNUAL CASH FLOW STATEMENT | |
|---|---|
| INCOMES | |
| Salary A | $ |
| Salary B | $ |
| Other: | $ |
| Other: | $ |
| TOTAL INCOME | $ |

| PRIMARY COMMITTED EXPENSES | |
|---|---|
| Mortgage | $ |
| Auto loan | $ |
| Student loan | $ |
| Credit card minimum payment | $ |
| Medical insurance | $ |
| Medical copays and deductibles | $ |
| Auto insurance | $ |
| Home insurance | $ |
| Utility bills (electric, gas, water, trash) | $ |
| Grocery bills | $ |
| Auto fuel | $ |
| Auto maintenance | $ |
| Basic clothing | $ |
| Personal care | $ |
| Homeowners' association dues | $ |
| Other: | $ |
| Other: | $ |
| TOTAL PRIMARY COMMITTED | $ |

| SECONDARY COMMITTED EXPENSES | |
|---|---|
| Home/cell phones | $ |
| Internet service | $ |
| Alarm system | $ |
| Home repair | $ |
| Pet expenses | $ |
| Charitable giving | $ |
| Other: | $ |
| Other: | $ |
| **TOTAL SECONDARY COMMITTED** | $ |

| TAXES | |
|---|---|
| Federal income tax | $ |
| State income tax | $ |
| Social Security tax | $ |
| Medicare tax | $ |
| Property tax | $ |
| Vehicle tax | $ |
| Other: | $ |
| **TOTAL TAXES** | $ |
| **TOTAL COMMITTED EXPENSES & TAXES** | $ |
| **AVAILABLE FUNDS FOR SAVING/ DISCRETIONARY SPENDING** | $_____<br>Total Income – (Committed Expenses + Taxes) |

| SAVINGS / PROTECTION GOALS | |
|---|---|
| Retirement (15% savings goal) | $ |
| Education | $ |
| Protection | $ |
| Major purchase: | $ |
| Major purchase: | $ |
| **TOTAL SAVINGS / PROTECTION** | $ |

| DISCRETIONARY SPENDING | |
|---|---|
| Dining and recreation | $ |
| Vacations | $ |
| Gym memberships | $ |
| Gifts to family | $ |
| TV/video streaming service | $ |
| **TOTAL DISCRETIONARY SPENDING** | $ |
| **REMAINING CASH FLOW** | $ |

# Your Top-Down Cash Flow Breakdown

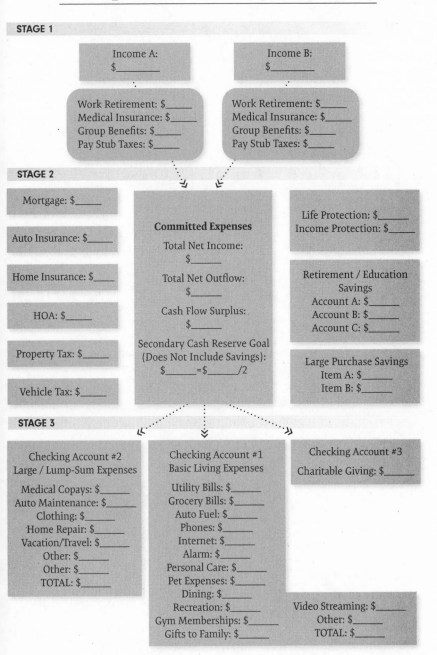

**STAGE 1**

Income A:
$_____

Income B:
$_____

Work Retirement: $_____
Medical Insurance: $_____
Group Benefits: $_____
Pay Stub Taxes: $_____

Work Retirement: $_____
Medical Insurance: $_____
Group Benefits: $_____
Pay Stub Taxes: $_____

**STAGE 2**

Mortgage: $_____

Auto Insurance: $_____

Home Insurance: $_____

HOA: $_____

Property Tax: $_____

Vehicle Tax: $_____

**Committed Expenses**

Total Net Income:
$_____

Total Net Outflow:
$_____

Cash Flow Surplus:
$_____

Secondary Cash Reserve Goal
(Does Not Include Savings):
$_____=$_____/2

Life Protection: $_____
Income Protection: $_____

Retirement / Education
Savings
Account A: $_____
Account B: $_____
Account C: $_____

Large Purchase Savings
Item A: $_____
Item B: $_____

**STAGE 3**

Checking Account #2
Large / Lump-Sum Expenses

Medical Copays: $_____
Auto Maintenance: $_____
Clothing: $_____
Home Repair: $_____
Vacation/Travel: $_____
Other: $_____
Other: $_____
TOTAL: $_____

Checking Account #1
Basic Living Expenses

Utility Bills: $_____
Grocery Bills: $_____
Auto Fuel: $_____
Phones: $_____
Internet: $_____
Alarm: $_____
Personal Care: $_____
Pet Expenses: $_____
Dining: $_____
Recreation: $_____
Gym Memberships: $_____
Gifts to Family: $_____

Checking Account #3

Charitable Giving: $_____

Video Streaming: $_____
Other: $_____
TOTAL: $_____

# ABOUT GREG PLITT

Gregory Plitt Jr. (1977–2015) was an actor, model, entrepreneur, and motivational speaker. He appeared on more than 250 magazine covers as an elite male fitness model and spoke to millions of people about fitness, nutrition, and motivation through seminars and expos, television segments, and videos on his website. He educated clients on the integration of mental and physical health, sharing real experiences and life lessons.

Greg's brand affiliations included MET_Rx nutrition, Under Armour Performance Apparel, Gold's Gym, Old Spice, Dodge Ram Trucks, and ESPN. His film credits include *The Good Shepherd* with Robert De Niro and *Terminator Salvation* with Christian Bale, and he had recurring roles on Bravo's *Workout*, HGTV's *Designed to Sell*, and NBC's *Days of Our Lives*.

Prior to his fitness and entertainment career, Greg graduated from the United States Military Academy at West Point and served as a US Army Ranger and as a company commander in charge of more than 180 soldiers. He was a two-time All-American and three-time state champion wrestler in Maryland, a professional skydiver with more than 2,500 jumps, and a golf club champion. "I have always been one who chooses the path less traveled when facing a crossroads in life," Greg wrote. "I feel each and every one of us has a true potential inside that will be revealed only when we are challenged and face our fears."

Greg's legacy endures through his professional website (http://gregplitt.com) and Facebook page (https://facebook.com/gregplittpage).

# ACKNOWLEDGMENTS

Writing this book has been an emotional journey, and I could not have completed it without the incredible support of many individuals. First and foremost, I thank my cousin Greg for giving me the inspiration, the willpower, and the emotional guidance to see this project to its end. Greg's legacy will always live on in my heart, and I will do all that I can to share his powerful messages of hope and personal drive with generations to follow. To the Plitt and Teti families, thank you for allowing me to write this book and share Greg's story.

To my wife, Laura, thank you for your patience and support over these past three years. All of the late nights dedicated to research, writing, and editing would not have been possible without you believing in me and knowing the passion that I have for this project.

To my editor, Sarah, you helped turn what was an unstructured dream into a concrete reality. You have been so much more than an editor to me through this journey. Your professionalism is beyond compare, and I can say with great confidence that the product we created reflects the professional high standard that I could have achieved only with your help! Thank you for all of your honest feedback and your drive to always go beyond expectations!

To my colleague James, these past few years you have shown me the true meaning of embracing life and not allowing circumstances to dictate your direction in life. You have been a source of inspiration and reflection. I am grateful for the words of wisdom you have shared with me both personally and professionally.

To Greg's videographer, Mark, thank you for all the work that you did during Greg's life and the work you continue to do to support his legacy. *Owning the Dash* would never have come into existence if it was not for the videos you created! Greg was lucky to know you, and your videos help to ensure his legacy never dies.

To all of the individuals and families who provided feedback on the book, thank you for your time and insight. A very big thank you to Blake, Tim, Pam, Karin, Gail, Jane, Jason, Madhav and Ratna, Brandon and Alecia, David and Laura, John and Jenelle, Paul and Katy, Vinny and Joy, Kevin and Heather, Jamie and Laura, Tom and Francie, Perry and Gail, and Matt and Kelly. Thank you also to my family—Mom, Dad, Kathy, Matt, and all of my cousins—and to my colleagues Debbie, Sherry, Jason, Hunter, and Todd.

Finally, thank you to Nina, Michelle, Ben, and everyone at Mascot Books who helped me with the final stages of this project. Your insight and professionalism are much appreciated!

# INDEX